WHAT PE(SAYING...

The man is quite possibly certifiable insane
but is undeniably a brilliant tutor
Student Feedback

An actuary, with a sense of humour?
Inconceivable!
Vizzini[*]

The farce is strong in this one.
Darth Vader

New phone. Who dis?
The Actuarial Profession

---

[*] This joke requires knowledge of "The Princess Bride". If your parents never introduced you to this masterpiece then I can give you the number of a good lawyer.

CONFESSIONS
OF AN
ACTUARIAL
TUTOR

OTHER BOOKS BY THE AUTHOR

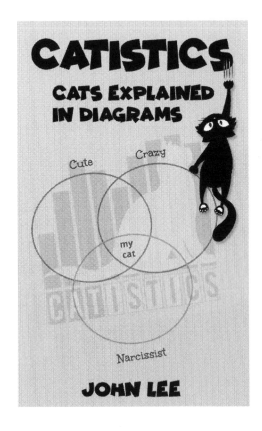

CONFESSIONS

OF AN

ACTUARIAL

TUTOR

ANECDOTES, JOKES & GENERAL GEEKINESS

JOHN LEE

Published by:

Kingdom Collective Publishing

Unit 10936, PO Box 6945
London, W1A 6US
kingdomcollectivepublishing@gmail.com

Book and Cover design by 100covers
Editing by Katherine.
ISBN: 978-1-912045-86-0

First Edition: November 2019

DEDICATION

This little book is for all the many students I've taught over the years. Without you I would just be standing in a room talking to myself. Admittedly, sometimes even with you there is little difference, but now is not the place to mention that.

CONTENTS

INTRODUCTION

A long time ago in a classroom far,

far away…

DISCLAIMER

The lawyers tell me that it's important to state that the opinions in this book do not reflect those of the Actuarial Profession nor those of my employer.

Hollywood would say that this book is "inspired by a true story," but in my case it would be better labelled as "loosely based on John's reality." This means that for the stories that are based on fact, I've taken the liberty of exaggeration to try and make my life seem more interesting than it actually is. It's one of the things we actuaries do to avoid despair over our dull lives.

The names of the students contained in this book have been removed to protect their anonymity or because I simply can't remember them. With the exception of Ross, whose name is included in this book as part of my penance for embarrassingly forgetting it in a tutorial after he brought me chocolate[1].

---

[1] Though admittedly he did buy it as part of his apology for turning up to my tutorial without his actuarial tables nor his calculator nor anything that would facilitate him to work.

TRIGGER WARNING

This is meant to be a satirical comedy book. As such, I will be poking fun at many aspects of life, though I'll mostly be targeting us actuaries as well as accountants, but that's only fair given the teasing accountants give us actuaries[2].

If you are of a sensitive disposition and easily offended then this sentence is your trigger warning: I have Asperger's and therefore I do have difficulty discerning the line between funny and rude[3]. I often stay awake at night wondering why there's a linear function dividing funny and rude in the first place.

---

[2] The standard joke accountants make about actuaries is that we don't have the personality to be an accountant. That's just plain wrong. We don't have the personality for many jobs, not just accountancy. But on a serious note, my friend and mentor is an accountant and this is all just part of the banter between us so please don't take anything I say seriously.

[3] Notice how I cunningly avoid responsibility for my actions by blaming it on a condition? Also makes those complaining about me look like they're picking on someone with a disability and I get to play the victim card.

GLOSSARY FOR AMERICAN READERS

As an English actuary I speak the Queen's English and drink cups of tea. To help those from our rebellious colony make sense of our British actuarial world I offer the following brief glossary:

Actuarial terms

101/CT3	Exam P/1 but without multi-choice
102/CT1	Exam FM/2 but without multi-choice
108/CT2/CB1	VEE Accounting and Finance
106/CT6	bits of STAM and SRM (Exam 5)
CM1	Exam FM/2 and bits of LTAM
CS1	Exam P/1 and bits of STAM and SRM (Exam 5) and PA
CS2	bits of LTAM, STAM and SRM (Exam 5) and PA
CA1/CP1	the third level of hell described in 50 chapters
CA3/CP3	similar to DMAC but with beautiful style, elocution and the Queen's English.
IFoA	Institute and Faculty of Actuaries – like the SoA or CAS but with a Latin motto which no-one recalls.

Non-actuarial terms

Anti-clockwise	*counterclockwise* but with 5-8 hour time difference
Apologise	*apologize*, but with more grovelling
Biscuit	*cookie* but consumed more delicately, often with a

	little finger in the air.
Bourbons	abbreviation for *bourbon biscuits*, which according to Wikipedia is a "sandwich style biscuit consisting of two thin rectangular dark chocolate–flavoured biscuits with a chocolate buttercream filling." If that doesn't make you want to become British then nothing will.
Digestive	abbreviation of *digestive biscuits* – the closest thing in America would be Graham's crackers, but even they would be sadly lacking.
Flies	*fly* or *zipper*, but usually never mentioned in public
Formulae	*formulas* but with Latin superiority
Gingernut	*ginger snap* except that we dip it in a cup of tea
Humour	*humor* but with added British dry wit
Lift	*elevator*, but with more awkward silences
Maths	*Math* but with an s, to show that we have far more of it over here in the UK...
One thousand million	American *billion*
Queue	line formed usually for no reason whatsoever, but never questioned
Rubbish	like garbage, but far less vulgar.
Secondary school	High School but with uniforms to demonstrate our superiority.
Sympathise	*sympathize* but with the offer of a cup of tea.
Tick	*checkmark* and not those creepy crawlies that keep us out of long grasses and forests.
Underground	subway but with people constantly telling you to "mind the gap."

PART 1

What's an actuarial tutor and the many other questions
I get asked

WHAT IS AN ACTUARIAL TUTOR?

Someone who tutors actuaries.

I'm glad to have cleared that up for you.

What do you mean, you don't know what an actuary is?

They are a mythical mathematical creature, rarer than a unicorn and twice as shy.

If you stand very still and look like a spreadsheet, you might be lucky enough to see one emerge from their office late at night, foraging for food. But this period is all too brief as they quickly head to their homes lest they have to engage in small talk with strangers.

As an actuarial tutor, I was trained in the mystical art of capturing young lesser spotted actuaries as they leave the safety of their nests. As part of my conservation work, I help prepare them to overcome the many trials, known as *actuarial exams*, that they will face in the wild.

Once they have demonstrated their prowess in my safe and controlled environment, I release them back into the wild.

Actuarial Tutors hope these fledglings will successfully navigate these trials so they can be welcomed into the adult pack of actuaries. There they can live out the rest of their lives in monochrome.

HOW DID I BECOME AN ACTUARIAL TUTOR?

As an actuarial tutor, people often say to me, "What are you doing in my garden?"

However, in tutorials, it's more common for students to ask how I ended up becoming an actuarial tutor.

Most of the time, they are only asking because they're trying to distract me from the fact that they don't want to do any work. Engaging me in conversation is the perfect ruse. But on the off chance that these humble students could actually be interested in my sad life, I tell them, "Too many drinks, a smack on the head from a sultry wench, and I ended up here."

However, more astute students realised that this may not be entirely the truth. Possibly my nose growing 12 inches like Pinocchio tipped them off. And so, pressing me for the real answer, reveals one that is sadly not quite as impressive:

I applied for the job.

I mean, how else does one find jobs?

It's like when people ask, "Where do you come from?" and

then are surprised when I reply, "From my mother and father." Is there some kind of alien seeding of the earth that I'm not aware of? Or maybe this whole stork bringing a baby thing isn't an old wives' tale after all.

Anyway, my wife spotted an advert for my current position and said, "This looks good." It shames me to say it, but in my ignorance, I asked her, "What's an actuary?"

Despite spelling the company's name wrong in the opening sentence of my cover letter, I received an interview which consisted of four parts:

- A 30-minute face-to-face interview in which I stated my weakness was perfectionism. Sadly, they didn't take the warning, thinking it was my clever way to avoid saying I had any weaknesses. They now realise their error.

- A 30-minute mock tutorial with about six other tutors who stood in as my students. They did their best to make me squirm by asking awkward questions. They seemed to enjoy their roleplay a tad too much methinks!

- A review and writing exercise where I had to find all the deliberate mistakes made in a chapter of notes[1]. Followed by writing new course notes on a particular topic.

- And finally, a written exercise where I outlined current developments in the educational field.

I was clearly writing far more than they expected in the exercises. They first shifted me from pen and paper to mouse and computer to speed me up. In the end, they just resorted to throwing me out into the street as they were ready for the next interviewee. "I really enjoyed that interview," I reflected as I lay there in the gutter. I was so pleased when they offered me the job! That is, until they told me that all the other interviewees had turned it down[2]. But beggars can't be choosers.

Some months later, I met one of the other interviewees. He was one of the students in a tutorial I was teaching. It wasn't awkward at all when he bitterly revealed, "I applied for the job you got." No, there was absolutely no pressure at all on my

---

[1] Including a pesky error in the footer which I missed.

[2] Only joking! I mean, who would turn down such a great job? I tell you, I signed and returned that contract faster than you can say antidisestablishmentarianism before they realised their mistake.

teaching abilities that day. Excuse me while I step outside to weep a moment.

ARE YOU A "PROPER" ACTUARY THEN?

Given that extensive modelling has shown that the combination of taking 15 actuarial exams and working in an office are 99.7% effective at crushing the soul out of people, students may suspect I may not be a proper actuary. I appear to still have a sense of humour.

But really, it's just an excuse they use to justify asking a rather personal question. I mean, they might as well ask me for my age and weight.

HOW OLD ARE YOU AND WHAT DO YOU WEIGH?

Absolutely no idea.

SO, ARE YOU A PROPER ACTUARY OR NOT?

The game's up. Sherlock's going to be out of a job! I tried using my advanced methods of distraction but you still noticed I hadn't actually answered the question. Or perhaps you didn't notice and just happened to read the previous sentence and then took the undeserved credit.

Either way, I confess it was me in the study with the candlestick[3].

The truth is: I taught maths, stats, and finance in secondary school to children from 11 to 18 years of age, and then I took some exams before becoming a tutor.

I quickly add, "But yes, I passed all the exams and am therefore fully qualified," to prevent students rising up against this imposter in their midst.

---

[3] For those who are confused by the previous sentence I'm referring to the board game "Cluedo" ("Clue" for my American readers) not some dubious activity actuaries undertake in the study with household equipment and a dead body.

WHY DID YOU LEAVE TEACHING?

Well now, I've opened up a whole area ripe for further exploration. Seeing as they're on a roll of distracting me further, (I mean taking an interest in my sad life), they usually follow up with this question.

Anyone who asks an ex-teacher why they left teaching has absolutely no idea about the teaching profession. Whereas anyone who has been a teacher or is married to one will immediately sympathise with me. The only question the latter group want to ask is how long did I last? It's kind of a measure of my Bear Grylls educator survival ability.

You think surviving in a desert with no food or water is challenging? Try getting teenagers interested in maths.

Been there done that, bought the T-shirt, and underwent the PTSD counselling. As the counselling is not quite complete. I still flinch every time a student raises a hand as I get flashbacks of sharp objects being hurled at me.

HAVE YOU THOUGHT ABOUT BECOMING A PROPER ACTUARY?

I'm never sure how to take this question. Are they implying that my teaching is so bad that I should look for another career? Or are they jealous that I still have personality and are seeking the means to destroy it forever?

Or maybe they're concerned about how I'm missing out on more money as a proper actuary? That's rather like my dad who, when he learnt what "proper" actuaries in London earn, said, "John, you could earn £****** as an actuary!" To which I replied, "That's a fascinating fact, my dearest father. And your point is?"

His assumption being that earning more money is better. In which case, becoming a dictator of a small country would clearly make me the favourite son.

But there's actually more to life than earning money.

I apologise, I should have told you to sit down before I dropped that bombshell.

For it's not until you have nearly lost something (and no, spreadsheet macros do not count) that you realise what really is important.

In my case, it was nearly losing my wife to suicide from clinical postnatal depression that woke me up to that stark truth.

Apologies, I should have told you to stay seated before dropping that truth bomb in this supposedly amusing book of anecdotes. After all, you didn't pick up this book to hear sob-stories but I understand if the emotional impact makes you wish to help out in some way. In which case, I'm very happy to accept bitcoin donations. Or chocolate. Both work well for me.

Anyway, I digress.

We were talking about me considering becoming a "proper" actuary and what better way to illustrate my issue than to recall an actual conversation with an actuarial head-hunter.

You know; those people who live in jungles and hunt for the heads of actuaries to put on poles as a warning to others. It's rumoured they are distant relatives of accountants.

So, there I was sitting in the office when this head-hunter rings me up. "Hi John, this is Jeff."

Okay, so his name might have been something other than Jeff, but I'm old and can't remember that piece of information as it really wasn't relevant to me passing my exams. Actually, neither was the rest of the conversation which just goes to show how my mind works. Anyhow, the point is that I didn't know him from Adam, except that his name wasn't Adam. Though it might have been as my memory of this unimportant piece of information has long since gone.

"Hello Jeff, this is John." I replied, returning his rather presumptuous use of my first name. I mean, not even my kids get to call me John.

"So, how are you doing in your studies?" The conversation started innocently enough. It quickly progressed to, "What are you looking for in your actuarial career?" Presumably, he was hoping that I would express some kind of longing that coincidentally would be fulfilled by a position that he just happened to be seeking actuaries to fill. Or maybe he had developed a new spreadsheet function that was set to revolutionise my life.

Well, I thought, I could blow him off or I could play his game, and so I replied, "I like that my current job in not London based, and 9 to 5 means 9 to 5 and that I can flex my hours to fit round my family. Mostly I like not being stuck in an office."

"Oh! Okay." he stammered – clearly he was not used to someone having a list of requirements, or maybe he wasn't used to someone that didn't just say, "I can't talk right now." Head-hunters don't seem to realise that ringing you in the office of your current employer is not really conducive to having a conversation about leaving said job.

He then mentioned something about getting back to me. As it's been more than 10 years now, I'm starting to lose hope of ever finding another job that's like my current one. It just makes me feel like I should just give up searching and become an accountant instead.

Okay maybe that joke was taken too far.

Suffice to say, there exists no other actuarial job that meets the work-life balance that is important to me.

And so, it seems that I am destined to never become a real actuary. I'll just have to content myself with dressing up and pretending to be one instead.

JOHN LEE | 27

WHY DON'T THEY EMPLOY QUALIFIED ACTUARIES RATHER THAN TEACHERS?

The company I work for does. Actuaries are absolutely essential for the later subjects which require real world experience. However, let's just say that actuaries that become tutors are clear outliers both in the ability to communicate and the personality distribution curves for actuaries. A null hypothesis of "is an actuary" based on these attributes and tested on actuarial tutors would be rejected at the 0.01% level.

Why else do you think that the one actuarial exam with the lowest pass rate is in Communication?

Nowhere is this more evident than in the mock tutorials that are run as part of the interview process. I now get to play the role of a student at some of these tutorials. I can tell you that I'm often struggling to stay awake and I'm really trying. Real actuarial students wouldn't stand a chance.

I also like to play the student who complains, "But I don't understand," preferably in a whiney voice, just to see how the potential tutor handles explaining things to mere mortals. I remember one candidate who replied with something like this, "It's obvious!", to my question. As far as I was concerned it was all over. But I'm sure they'd have a great career as a lecturer at university.

IS THIS YOUR FULL-TIME JOB?

Again, I'm not sure how to take this question.

I sometimes wonder if this is a polite way of saying, "Don't give up your day job." But yes, I assure them that being an actuarial tutor is indeed my full-time job.

SO WHAT DO YOU DO WHEN YOU'RE NOT TEACHING?

Well they hang us back up in a cupboard until we're needed again to save the actuarial world from the forces of evil.

Sadly, as much as I would like to think that answer is true it's not. There isn't a cupboard in our office and our filing cabinets are just too small.

So instead I give the answer: "Sit around, drink coffee, and shoot pool."

Sadly, this is not true either, as there isn't a pool table. Nor chairs. But I do lots of writing, updating and reviewing materials, and I have various other jobs like that to do.

Wait! Where are you all going? Come back!

I'll stop talking about these mundane matters and move onto something more interesting. Such as the mysteriously strong correlation between me saying I'm going to be in the office on a particular day and the other tutor's absence on that same day. They assure me this is purely coincidental, as is their presence in the office on the days I'm not in.

I often work at home in my little study. However, my four kids and my cats, Spartapuss and Cleocatra, make that somewhat difficult. I can't understand why...

To be fair, if the cats weren't there then that space would be filled with something else. It's part of my 'diffusion filing' system. By spreading everything over every surface, logically anything you want is closer to the surface and thus easier to find. Sadly, despite the theory being sound, empirical evidence doesn't appear to back it up. But I remain convinced that my diffusion filing model is correct. I just need more data. At least, that's what I tell my wife.

I can't fathom why the HR department deemed my work environment unsuitable when I submitted this photo as part of my H&S assessment. I suspect perhaps it had something to do with not using a screen protector or something along those lines. It's times like this that Photoshop comes in handy.

WHAT OTHER SUBJECTS DO YOU TEACH?

I like maths. There's something so satisfying about working through a problem and getting the right answer at the end, fist punching the air, and doing that little celebratory happy dance.

You just don't get that with words. Which is probably why, as an actuarial student, I shot through the earlier mathematical actuarial exams, and then lost the will to live when I studied later subjects where equations became an endangered species.

I was happily teaching the mathematical subjects of CT1, CT3 and CT6 when my boss said to me one day, "Hey John, wouldn't you like to teach CT2?"

I'm positive that Business Finance (CB1)/ Finance and Financial Reporting (CT2/108) have been designed by the Profession to help actuaries realise why they wisely chose not to become accountants.

Indeed, if boredom were a tangible asset, then writing this exam would make me a rich man. Watching paint dry would win out in a zero-sum strategy game using minimax or a

Bayesian criterion for decisions.

I remember as a student revising and then waking up with my face stuck to my notes and drool on my chin. I'm surprised doctors are not recommending this subject as a cure for insomnia.

In fact, the audio revision product for this subject is the only one to carry a warning, "Do not drive or operate heavy machinery whilst listening to this product."

I suspect this removes the threat of a large liability from students who sue after falling asleep at the wheel whilst listening to this product.

So I replied to my boss, "You're right, I wouldn't."

To which he answered, "Very good! CA1/CP1 it is then."

Methinks I walked into a trap there...

Students who attended my tutorials know that I tried. Dear God, I tried. I felt like a spy trying to sneak book work into their brains when they weren't looking. I tried to garner their attention through real-life examples and to keep them awake by setting the evil questions from the handout.

But the hardest part about teaching this subject was that the students had trouble differentiating between realising that it was the subject that was boring and not me.

DO YOU MARK ASSIGNMENTS?

Occasionally, I do mark assignments that students send in. I love helping students by finding where the problem is and pointing them in the right direction. However, it takes so long to do this well that I can lose the plot, ending up stabbing myself in the eye with a pen.

There have been some scripts that restored my faith in the total depravity of students. One year, there was a student script for CA1/CP1 which was word for word identical with the solutions. Frankly, I think it would have saved them time if they had just photocopied the solutions. However, I still marked their work thoroughly and discovered within all its 10 pages that there was exactly one place where the script and solution differed.

The student had corrected a minor grammatical error.

Of course, I thanked them for their help in improving the quality of the assignments. Silver lining level up.

DO YOU MARK EXAM SCRIPTS?

Yes, I do mark for the Profession. I know, I know! I just said that marking makes me want to stab myself in the eye but you can't rule out madness.

I kind of fell into it. A marker for 102/CT1/CM1 dropped out at the very last minute and I offered to step in as that's the kind of person I am, especially when I'm getting paid for helping out. You must understand, the Profession was desperate or they would never have considered me otherwise.

Marking for the Profession is a volunteer position which does come with a little remuneration, as we markers value intangible assets, such as love and prestige, more highly.

However, marking does require sacrificing evenings and weekends for about a month. For me, it's worth it to give something back to the Profession. The extra money helps fund writing little books like this one – because let's face it, I'm hardly likely to turn a profit as an author.

My eldest son questioned me on my strange behaviour one

day[4]: "Dad, why do you do marking? You spend so many evenings and weekends marking!"

"I do it to earn some pocket money," I replied, in that smug way only actuarial fathers can when explaining things to their non-actuarial children.

"But you use it to pay for publishing your books, which means you spend more evenings and weekends busy writing them."

Darn. He was cleverer than I gave him credit for. It was time to come clean.

"You do not understand the power of the dark side of the mid-life crisis, my son."

"But father, there's good in you; I feel it."

"No, it is too late for me, my son."

However, I took his concerns to heart and decided it was best to stop marking financial mathematics, where scripts could take up to an hour to mark even when they only scored 1% in total. I'm now marking subjects where students give up more quickly. Ahem.

---

[4] The truth is, he questions my strange behaviour every day – but this particular day he was questioning my strange marking behaviour.

WHAT TRAINING DO YOU UNDERGO TO BECOME AN ACTUARIAL TUTOR?

The ancient art of actuarial tutor training is a tightly guarded secret that is only revealed to candidates who prove themselves worthy. In my case, they just felt rather sorry for me and taught me a couple of things regardless.

The training, which has been carefully passed down through the ages, begins with the mystical art of finding your inner actuarial model from which all assumptions flow. Once found, you are then taught how to manipulate its assumptions so you can develop what the world, in its naivety, calls superpowers but are actually just consequences of your updated model. Sadly, I was unable to achieve this so they just taught me how to cope with disappointment in a world that doesn't conform to any model I construct.

The more traditional aspects of training seek to develop the physical and mental abilities of candidates to the point they can withstand the rigours of non-stop tuition:

- Weight training to carry laptops to tutorials, rearrange tables in the classrooms, and develop rippling muscles to intimidate any accountants that try to sneak into the room.

- A special keto/Mediterranean/Atkins/5-2 diet to develop immunity to the various coughs, colds, and other infections that students attempt to share with us during tutorials.

- Memory training to memorise student's names, critical values from the Z, t, chi squared and F distributions, what page of the tables each of the formulae are on, and how many times each topic has been covered in the past papers.

- First responder engineering to fix problems at venues including wobbly tables, broken lights, windows that won't stay open, and issues with IT.

- Grief counselling to help students who suddenly realise the never-ending life of study that they have committed themselves to.

- Clinical psychology to learn how to use sarcasm to coax an introverted actuary to talk.

- Oh, and some training in maths, statistics, R programming, and Excel.

Upon completion of this training, actuarial tutors receive a utility belt to store their tables, calculator, mechanical pencil, red pen, and defibrillator. Sadly, I didn't complete the training and only received a brown paper bag which just doesn't carry the same street cred.

PART 2

A tutorial, a tutorial,
my kingdom for a tutorial!

Face to Face Tutorials
REGULARS AND BLOCKS

Actuarial students in the UK get day release for good behaviour so that they can attend tutorials that are held at venues around the country.

Like everything you buy these days, there is a multiplicity of types of tutorial to appeal to every conceivable type of actuary.

The standard face-to-face tutorial offered is affectionately known as the regular. And rightly so. as this reminds you of an older person eating bran for breakfast for reasons best not mentioned in the pages of a book of this calibre.

Regulars consist of a number of tuition days spread out over the session, allowing students to recover before the next onslaught. We'd like to think that students take these so they can divide their studies into more manageable parts. The reality is, they just space their cramming until the weekend directly before each tutorial. But I pray that these students will, in time, master the art of regular study, avoiding facing the hard truth that they have no social life, or indeed friends.

These days of tuition are full days, but many years ago, I taught half-days. Let's just say that the afternoon tutorials where students arrived to class after a morning at work meant they were already exhausted. I remember teaching 106/CT6/CS2 regularly on Friday afternoons. While I might say I was teaching, I think it was more of a case of me trying to forcefully pour information down their throats while they gagged. It was entertaining until the police came.

The other kind of tutorials are called blocks which consist of a block of consecutive teaching days, usually much closer to the exam. These can be thought of as the constipated version of tuition, and in a similar way to actual constipation, require some form of gritting one's teeth to overcome.

Now, all these face-to-face tutorials are held in venues around the country. You might be tempted to think of my job as glamorous, travelling around teaching in places such as London, Reading, Bristol, Manchester, Leeds, Dublin, and Birmingham. As I'm based in the south of England, most of my tutorials are in London, the home of our beloved queen.

I discovered I have a map in my drawer of Liverpool, so I must have taught there at some point in the past. But I have no recollection of this whatsoever. Perhaps the trauma of visiting this city has caused me to blank out my trip. Or maybe I never went there but I just like collecting maps for towns that I have no desire to visit.

Some of the places I visit are not quite as glamorous as you may have first thought. And to be honest I really only get to see the inside of the local office and when you've seen one office you've pretty much seen them all.

Face-to-face tuition

PRIVATE TUITION

I've also done a little private tutoring for students. In all honesty, I should have stopped most of those tutorials after 5 minutes, the time it took to discover the sizable gap between their knowledge and what was required to pass the actuarial exams.

Perhaps they asked me to tutor because they knew I'm a Christian and I believe in miracles. But I can tell you that my faith was sorely tested and I longed to simply say to them, "Save your money. You ain't gonna pass."

One student was due to sit their 102/CT1/CM1 exam (FM for my American readers) a couple of weeks after our session. They had absolutely no idea what on earth a present value was. It took great effort to maintain my outward composure even though inwardly there was much weeping and gnashing of teeth.

Non face-to-face tuition
ONLINE TUTORIALS

What better way to teach students in far flung places than having a live *online* tutorial? This kind of tuition has the added bonus of reducing student actuaries' social anxiety - they don't have to sit in close-proximity to other people. Presumably, they could even take this kind of tutorial sitting at home on their sofa in their pyjamas[9].

Now whilst the feedback from students on these tutorials is quite positive, I confess I often feel like I'm some kind of talk radio DJ making conversation and jokes with only the occasional "lol" in the chat box as an indicator people are out there listening.

So, to liven things up a bit, I include silly responses in polls that I set:

---

[9] Fortunately, students don't use their webcams which saves rather a lot of awkwardness all-round.

What is your progress on the CS1 material?

○ I have a confession

○ I have read all the material but I haven't done any questions

○ I have read all the material and have done some questions

○ I have read all the material, done all the questions and am silently judging those who haven't

But despite the interactive nature of these tutorials, there's always that one student who writes nothing at all. Not in the public chat box, not through private answers to questions I put out there.

Nothing. At. All.

I get worried. What if they have died and there I am, insensitively asking them to answer questions whilst they quietly decompose on the sofa.

I cannot let this happen, and I ask out loud, "If you're alive out there, could you just write something in the chat box now?"

Nothing.

Now, it's generally known that actuaries, particularly when in the office, exhibit symptoms that can be mistaken for death. Vacant looks, white pallor and the inability to answer simple

JOHN LEE | 51

questions, for example. Even so, they are still quite proficient at responding to emails and text messages.

My suspicions have been confirmed. They are DEAD.

At least that's the node in my healthy-sickness-death model categorises them as. The question then becomes: How do I record this on my attendance sheet? Does watching a tutorial whilst dead still count as being present?

Non face-to-face tuition

ONLINE CLASSROOM

As IFoA exams are taken by students around the world, most are not able to attend face-to-face tuition. Time zones often make attendance at live online tutorials difficult. I must salute the student who was up at 4am to listen to me teach live. Hence, pre-recorded tutorials are made available via an 'online classroom'.

Some students watch these videos prior to attending a face-to-face tutorial[10] and upon hearing my voice, exclaim "You're one of the tutors in the videos!" Just in case you're worried about my students' observational skills, they only hear my voice in an online classroom. I narrate the videos used in those pre-recorded sessions in my 'actuarial voice.' Coincidently, it sounds a bit like the voice I used when reading bedtime stories to my children. Though those stories had less maths and more plot:

"In this unit, we will be covering Little Red Riding Hood. I'm probably sending you to sleep right now as I read this in

---

[10] I think they hope, by just listening, they don't have to read the notes but have someone do it for them. I would never accuse them of such a thing. Oh no.

gentle, dulcet tones. Soon you will be under my control and you will make a large payment to the following Swiss bank account."[11]

Any delusions of fame on my part are quickly destroyed when they tell me that they listen to me at 1.5 times speed. In fact, one student went as far as to confess that they listened to me at twice the normal speed. Given that they still recognised my normal voice I can only conclude that I sound like a chipmunk.

---

[11] If you want to hear the actuary voice, then you'll have to listen to the audiobook version.

THE FOUR SEASONS OF ACTUARIAL TEACHING

The work of an actuarial tutor is seasonal as I go through each six-month exam period. The four seasons are:

- Spring – Hope is in the air as the buds of the exams are visible on the Professions website. Tutors emerge from hibernation, foraging for new students to teach once or twice a week.

- Summer – Tutors are in full bloom, teaching two or three times a week with small groups of happy students with smiles on their faces. The thought of the exam season being near has yet to dawn on them.

- Autumn – Actuarial students are anxious, tutors are exhausted, and they shed their sanity whilst teaching four days a week. This season is the classic time when tutors become ill. For example, I once damaged my vocal cords so severely I couldn't talk properly in tutorials. It was then that I earned the nickname, 'The Actuarial Whisperer.'

- Winter – Exam season is upon the students. Tutors hibernate in the office, surviving on a stash of throat sweets and vitamin C tablets they gathered during the summer season.

PART 3

A day in the life of a tutor:

The beginning

GETTING THERE

Let me describe a typical day teaching a tutorial in London: I begin my journey a stone's throw from Oxford, in the heart of the Cotswolds.

Doesn't it sound idyllic?

Well, it would be, if it weren't for two issues:

Firstly, it has to be the furthest place in the UK from any beach. A kid's sandpit and paddling pool in the garden just doesn't hit the spot.

Secondly, it's just plain flat. Its so-called rolling hills just aren't proper mountains. I know it's a bit hypocritical of me criticising them for not being 'proper' when I'm not even a 'proper' actuary. Suffice to say, I spend a lot of time in Wales to rectify this issue[12].

When I'm teaching in London, I hop on my motorbike about 6:20 am to head to the Oxford train station. When I say motorbike, that's a rather generous term for my Jet14 125cc engine mounted on two wheels and a bit of plastic. Let's just

---

[12] The hills issue not the actuarial one.

say that it makes a push bike look like a Ferrari. However, I take great satisfaction overtaking Ferraris (the actual ones – not the push bike ones) stuck in the rush hour traffic, though my satisfaction is slightly dampened when it's tipping with rain.

From Oxford, I catch the 7.52am train to London Paddington which is a 50-minute journey. I say it takes 50 minutes but that makes an assumption that the train's actual journey time bears some resemblance to the published timetable. Based on extensive evidence gathered over the last 15 years of commuting, I can say with 95% confidence that chaos theory is a better model of the actual journey times.

Whilst on the train, I join with my fellow commuters, all secretly hoping to get a double seat to ourselves. In general, the British are loathe to communicate with strangers. Actuaries' fear of such communication is multiplied tenfold. Most commuters take the classic approach, leaving their bag on the seat next to them or pretending to be asleep whilst stretched across both seats. But commuters who board at Reading Station are not fooled by such paltry measures. I believe I have formulated a far superior method of making sure I have as much personal space as possible, based on reverse psychology.

As Reading Station commuters enter my train car, I look them in the eye and announce enthusiastically, "This seat's free! Come and sit here!" They quickly avert their eyes and scurry past me assuming I am some kind of pyscho. Sadly, I don't often get a chance to demonstrate the veracity of their assumption.

Occasionally, my reverse psychology backfires and attracts someone who is eager to chat with me on the way to work. But that's nothing that talking in detail about pensions can't solve. Soon I have them sleeping like a baby while I quickly make my getaway.

Once in London, I hop on the underground to take me to the nearest tube station to my destination. After 15 to 35 minutes of sniffing some stranger's armpit and listening to their music that is loud enough to stun small birds, I leave the tube for a short walk to the venue.

VENUES

Back in the day, I used to teach at any venue that wouldn't slam down the phone as soon as they heard I was an actuary (after, of course asking what an actuary was first and then discovering it involved mathematics).

My company must have been so desperate for venues one year that they booked a room in one of those modern avant-garde meeting places. The cosmetics company Lush was meeting next door if that gives you a mental image of the kind of place it was. The décor was nice but its stylish desks were the office desk equivalent of an evening handbag. These desks were created for image rather than any pretence of practicality. They weren't even big enough for a pad of paper. Students struggled to get a pencil case on them let alone anything else. As a result, my poor students were forced to work on their laps. You can only imagine how distraught the young OCD actuaries were when their writing implements went all over the place. It was also rather embarrassing as a tutor to spend the whole day looking at their laps to mark their work. But let's move on.

MAKING THE MOST OF VENUES

The advantage of teaching in venues such as hotels or meeting centres, aside from the biscuits (more on that later) is that they provide extras, such as pen and paper. Now extras are technically included in the price and so can't legitimately be called extras, but I digress.

Despite these extras being included in the tutorial fee, some students spurn such freebies by leaving them on the desks after the tutorial. Being environmentally conscious, I know that it is a waste to leave such items there. And so, I adopt them and take them home rather than toss them in the bin to prevent the turtles suffering from graphite poisoning or something like that.

When my children were younger, I used to give these freebies to them as gifts, which they loved. Now they're older, they realise what a cheapskate I am. I now place them in my study where my teens 'borrow' them but 'accidentally' forget to return them ever. It works well. The items are rehomed and my teenagers maintain their street cred by not accepting lame freebies directly from their father.

Over time, I realised that there are many other things included in the room that my company paid for that are going to waste. But as I'm unscrewing the light fixtures, I must confess that I wonder if I'm taking things a bit too far.

SETTING UP

I like to arrive at a venue at least an hour early so I can ensure that everything is set up and ready. Actuaries don't like surprises which could account for why we head to the office on Christmas day if we haven't purchased our own presents beforehand.

The room should have desks arranged in a U-shape with about 12 chairs around the outside. Unlike accountants who pack into classrooms like sardines, actuaries gather in small groups to facilitate individual feedback. Not that I've seen classroom packed full of sardines but I am an actuary and don't get out much. But I suspect that a packed room of accountants probably earn the same as our small group of actuaries so I guess there's actually some equality there.

In addition, a box containing blank name cards, question handouts, and their solutions should be in the room upon our arrival. But sometimes the venue thinks we actuaries have such boring lives that they try to help us to embrace our inner child by playing hide and seek with the box. If I am any indication, actuaries only get stressed by this game and there is little skipping around excitedly like small children.

My next task is to switch on my laptop, receiving the following urgent message as soon as I do: "Your mission, should you choose to accept it, is to connect your laptop to the projector and display it correctly before the tutorial starts. This message and laptop will self-destruct in 5 seconds."

Yes, *progression* meant moving from using flip charts as a medium of communication to using laptops. Flip charts are so last century, what with their pens or paper running out and, as one tutor group will vividly remember, having a tripod leg with a loose joint. Trying to teach whilst simultaneously stopping the flip chart from collapsing was one of the more challenging tasks that my tutor special ops training prepared me for.

Now with my advanced laptop, I only experience such minor issues as having no cable, having a cable but one that doesn't work, having a cable that works but a screen that doesn't, having a cable and screen that work but with an unknown reason why the two don't work together and a myriad of other complications that no training can ever prepare us for.

On the positive side, laptops are much easier to carry around in your bag than a flip chart.

Once these small issues are ironed out, I am free to perform my morning ablutions: ensuring that my biker "helmet hair" is tamed and the commuter grime is washed off of my face. Perhaps there might even be time for a quick shave. Shaving first thing in the morning before I'm properly awake has proved to be rather dangerous.

One venue I regularly teach at hasn't had hot water in over a year. I tried shaving once with cold water and let's just say that it certainly added a bit of colour to my boring white shirt.

With the room set up and my ablutions done, I take a moment to breath and mentally prepare myself for the task of trying to help introverted actuaries overcome their nature.

How do you spot the extrovert actuary at a party[13]?

He's the one staring at someone else's shoes.

At this point, it never fails. Just as I'm entering my happy place, a student arrives early. Well not just early, but EARLY early!

Initially, it's hard to tell whether they're exceptionally keen or whether they mistakenly believe the tutorial starts at 9 rather

---

[13] Yeah, I know that actuaries don't attend parties but it is one of the assumptions underlying this joke model. So let's just pretend that it's the compulsory office Christmas party and take it from there.

than 9.30. If it's the latter, within a few minutes, they'll look nervously around at the lack of other students. It only makes it worse when they realise they'll have to endure an additional 30 minutes of small talk from me before other students begin to arrive.

Sometimes it's all just too much for them so I'll have to display a picture of a spreadsheet to help the early bird recover from the trauma.

THE SMALLEST TUTORIAL GROUP EVER

As mentioned, tutorial groups are typically 10 to12 students. However, once I taught a group of only six students. The first student to arrive was at 9.20. Now if this had been the last tutorial in the series then that wouldn't have worried me. But usually on the first day of tutorial, students tend to arrive earlier, possibly to impress me with their keenness or just to scope out local coffee shops. But time ticked nervously on and at 9.30 none of the other students had turned up.

It seemed a bit silly starting with just one person, so I shot off an email to the other students to inquire how soon they'd arrive. I received replies from two students who explained that due to circumstances, they wouldn't be there that day. The three remaining students still had not yet arrived ten minutes later.

Now it may have been Thanos clicking his fingers but I wasn't going to wait any longer so I decided to start the tutorial with just one person. It was tricky trying to decide which student to ask which questions. But what made things more comical was the fact she had been out on the razz the night before. As she had a bit of a headache, she had hoped to escape answering any questions by hiding quietly amongst the other students in the class.

It was a cruel twist of fate. I can't remember at what time I eventually realised that no other students were going to arrive. It became increasingly silly teaching that one student sitting at a desk while I stood at the front writing on a flipchart. In the end, I just sat down next to her and wrote the notes on a piece of paper and gave her one-on-one help.

Despite getting a day's worth of private tuition, my lone student didn't seem very happy about it at all. I can't possibly think why.

GREETING STUDENTS

Students typically tend to walk into the room mumbling the standard British greeting of "Morning."

To which I reply, "Yes, it is. Well observed."

I take heart that these students are on the ball so much that they are able to notice the world around them. Not only that, they draw the appropriate conclusion about the time of day and then communicate that information succinctly to third parties. I rest assured that the tutorial is off to a promising start.

However, occasionally a student commits an actuarial faux pas of saying "Good morning!"

I mean, is it allowable for actuaries to say that at only 9 o'clock in the morning?

Surely this requires some sort of model to determine whether the morning can be called good. Since many of my students have only been up an hour or so, I have to question whether they have enough data to be able to draw that conclusion. Or are they basing their model on rather precarious assumptions?

Though there is a small part of me that wonders whether I'm

overthinking this whole greeting thing.

Finally, it should be mentioned that there is a small contingent of students who greet me with the unusual question: "CS1?"

To which I reply, "No, I'm John."

Dad joke level up

I mean, who would name their child after an actuarial exam? I guess if your parents were actuaries it could be the case. Which reminds me of the following actuarial joke:

A son asked his father, "Dad how did you decide on our names?"

The father replied, "Well, we named both of you after our favourite things. For example, your sister is called Rose as that's your mum's favourite flower. Why do you ask, VLookUp?"

STUDENTS' SEATING POSITIONS

It's interesting observing how students choose which desk to sit at around the U-shape. The first one to a tutorial usual chooses the prime location at the rear. They'll claim that this is because it affords the best view of the screen without having to twist their head – but it's really a smokescreen to cover the fact that they want to sit on the equivalent of the backrow in a classroom.

The second most favoured location is the desk nearest the door so the student can make a quick escape if asked to engage in conversation with others.

Subsequent students chose seats according to urinal positioning model. Apologies to the ladies who are bewildered by this analogy. That is, they space themselves out uniformly so as to avoid the faux-pas of actually sitting next to someone else until there is no other option. The only exception to this rule is where students work for the same company. Whilst they might not know each other that well, actuaries are reclusive beasts by nature, so the thought of sitting next to someone they have never met is more terrifying.

WHAT ABOUT SECOND TUTORIAL?

Actuaries are creatures of habit and always sit in exactly the same seats as before. On occasion, one student (usually the one who was late and had to sit next to me as a result) might mess things up by coming early and grabbing a prime location back row seat which causes untold anguish.

This manifests as a look of horror when the other students enter the room and observe the significant at 5% level change which forces them to reject the null hypothesis of 'same seat'. I've found that the disorientation can affect students for about 30 minutes afterwards.

REMEMBERING STUDENTS' NAMES

In order to complete the register and create an environment where no-one actually has to talk to each other to find out their name, I place blank name cards on the desks upon which the students can write their name[14]. Or somebody else's name – I don't mind as long as it's on the register.

However, the breed of name cards that I use are related to lemmings. During the tutorial, they throw themselves off table tops in a fit of pique. You can almost hear them saying, "I'd rather die than stay near these calculations." I do try and pick them up, but the floor seems a lot further away the older I get. It may be because I'm still growing.

But what about the next tutorial?

Unfortunately, part of British etiquette is to never ask someone their name after they told you once. It would just be so terribly rude to admit that they're so unimportant or dull that you've forgotten it. Usually we Brits easily resolve this

---

[14] Hence "name" cards. Should be obvious really – but us actuaries know never to assume anything!

problem by simply avoiding talking to that person ever again. However, for a tutor this is not really an option and using "you there" is not a particularly helpful way of indicating to whom your question is directed, as actuaries studiously avoid eye contact.

So, name cards are a social awkwardness life-saver. As actuarial students are such creatures of habit, if I gather the cards in the order the students sat round the U shape, I can then hand them out in the same order next session and give them to the correct student with only a few outliers. Result!

Alternatively, I could admit to struggling with names and scribble helpful notes next to their name on the register. Like "red hair", "looks like my cat" or "sounds like an accountant." When attendance sheets used to be on paper, this approach would be fine. Nowadays, they're a softcopy on the computer. Students may accidentally see these comments on the screen, which might be embarrassing to all parties involved. I have to admit, I'm nervous that a freedom of information access request would require the sharing of these little notes that their beloved tutor has written about them.

A fellow tutor resolves this issue by placing the name cards on the desks *before* the students arrived. This forced them to sit by their name – unless they fancied a name change – wait, they're actuaries! That would never happen. I was rather concerned that my colleague deliberately messed the order up to get students to sit next to different people. Some people just want to watch the world burn.

My favoured method is to leave the name cards near the entrance to the room hoping that the students will pick them up upon entering. Inevitably one student doesn't, and I'm then forced to either avoid asking them questions for that day, call them "you there", or attempt to guess which of the remaining cards left by the entrance is theirs.

Now, there are always those students who stand out because they form the outliers of your group of actuaries. They either willingly contribute to the tutorials at one end of the distribution or they studiously avoid doing any work at the other. It's much harder to remember the names of the generic students in the middle of the actuarial personality distribution. As regular tutorials are typically spaced 2 or 3 weeks apart and I teach a couple of other groups of students in between, it only adds to my quandary.

For some reason, I find it much easier to remember the girls' names rather than the boys. I worried that this was because I was some kind of perv until I was talking with a female colleague. She said she finds it easier to remember girls' names as well. Girls usually have very different hairstyles whereas boys all just have short hair. That's my excuse and I'm sticking to it.

So, I'm left with a handful of name cards to match to those generic male students and I'm too British to actually ask their names. Therefore, I opt to predict their names using a generalised linear model with covariates such as their seating position and my previous experience of what people with those names look like. Sadly, this model has resulted in me assigning a different name to someone and when they protested, I retorted that they don't look like their name.

Special shout out to Ross whom I called Jordan. Whilst this sort of thing happens a lot[15], I felt particular grieved at this faux pas because Ross had brought me chocolate during the previous tutorial. Because of my error, I scuppered my chances of him doing so again.

Once I have finally assigned names, even if they are assigned to the wrong student, I can at last fill out the register. That is, if I can remember the GDPR password for the Sensitive Data document. Fortunately, I have the foresight to store it in an obvious place so that I, and anyone hacking my computer, can

---

[15] Getting the wrong name that is, not calling every Ross I happen to meet Jordan.

quickly find it.

I mean if my register were to be leaked into the public domain there would be outcry at this abuse of data. This data could be used to blackmail students by threatening to tell other people that they're an actuary. As a result, they'd lose all their street cred and be forced to walk the streets wearing a sign saying "unclean". Or the data could be used to impersonate those students in order to illegally attend actuarial tutorials, take their question handouts, and sell them on the actuarial black-market.

I'm so glad the EU introduced the GDPR legislation. Without them, the consequences are truly terrifying.

TELL ME YOUR TROUBLES...

I could start a tutorial asking everyone to introduce themselves to each other, but the social anxiety caused by such a getting-to-know-you activity is likely to affect the students' performance for the rest of the day. Perhaps though, some students may be willing to sacrifice themselves if it helped them get to know potential hot dates and chat them up with an actuarial pick up line like, "My interest in you is compounding continuously."

Instead, I start by asking students where their problems lie. Despite me giving students a five-minute warning of this question, they still look like deer caught in the headlights when I eventually ask it. They then all stare at the list of topics on the board as if they've never seen them before.

A tense silence follows as everyone waits for someone else to go first.

Eventually, one brave student takes the plunge. It could be because I couldn't stand the waiting and nominated them to answer the question as they accidentally made eye contact just at the wrong moment.

Typically, they respond cautiously, nominating one chapter only.

This usually results in the rest of the group feeling more confident about nominating that same chapter. If they're all feeling brave, they might nominate an additional chapter as well.

It reminds me of that actuarial joke:

How many actuaries does it take to change a lightbulb?

How many did it take last time? Use that and maybe add a margin.

Case in point. They all copy the first response and maybe add a margin of an additional chapter.

HEALTH AND SAFETY

When I was a lad, we had something called *common sense*, but like many other natural resources, such as oil and gas, it is running low. Thus, causing us to move to another more renewable resource. And so, common sense has been replaced by its evil older twin, 'health and safety,' whose rules increase exponentially and therefore 'health and safety' is unlikely to become scarce.

For example, I remember as a child playing in an active building site. They were great fun and if we hurt ourselves and went running to our parents, they would reply with "Well, you shouldn't have been playing there."

Ah, the good old days.

Times have changed and 'health and safety' has arisen as the archenemy of testosterone.

Apparently, youngsters nowadays are not aware of the dangers of the world around them. Nowhere is this truer than in the world of young actuarial students who need to be educated about risk assessment. I mean, it's not like they'd learn this skill in their job.

Sadly, this means that at the beginning of a new tutorial series, I must point out what students should do in the event of a fire alarm:

"Should you hear a continuous ringing in your ears, it's possible you have tinnitus and should see your doctor. However, if everyone else also hears this same ringing, it's probably the signal to evacuate."

"Your nearest exit are the windows behind you. *indicates windows*. Your nearest safe exit are the stairs just outside the room. *indicates stairs*. I will wear this rather fetching fluorescent jacket *indicate fetching fluorescent jacket* and will lead you like the pied piper to our assembly point whereupon I shall do a head count. If one of you is missing, then I will run back into the burning building and save you from certain death. Such is my dedication as your tutor."

"Please do not stop to pick any items up except, of course, your actuarial tables. Do not use the lifts[16] as you sit at your desk all day pressing F9 and need the exercise anyhow. Should the nearest stairs be blocked, please administer yourself a laxative to increase your sense of urgency, before trying the next set of stairs."

---

[16] I don't say elevators as I'm British.

Now occasionally the students and I have the joy of experiencing a real fire...

...alarm test.

It's not as if the students have anything important to do, like passing exams. How could their time be better spent than by standing outside for 10 minutes waiting for someone to say "It's only pretend! You can come back in now!"

Special shout-out has to go my group in Birmingham who duly went outside into the sub-zero temperatures leaving all their worldly possessions inside[17], including their coats. Bless them, it took ages to thaw them out afterwards. The students that is – not the coats. The coats kept nice and cosy inside. I think a number of those students were actually tempted to start a real fire just to warm up.

Then there the time in West London where there was some sort of terrorist activity that police were trying to corner. So, they ordered us to evacuate the building, with all its security measures, and stand exposed on the green with all the people from all the other offices in the vicinity. I wasn't sure if the police were using us as bait to lure the terrorist into the open.

---

[17] Except their actuarial tables of course.

Certainly, it would have made the terrorist's job so much easier, all of us crowded together in one place rather than spread out in different buildings.

However, far more concerning than that was the time a fire alarm sounded at one venue. When I took the register of those lining up with me outside, I discovered that half of my tutor group was missing. At first, I wondered if they were testing me to see whether I really was serious about going back into the burning building to save them. But it was a fate even worse than a potential burning building that I saved them from. I found them queuing outside with accountants.

It's taken over 5 years of extensive PTSD counselling to recover from that dreadful day.

Finally, there was a fire alarm drill at a West London venue. We duly went out the back gate and stood at our designated point, which was just round the corner. We then waited to be told that we could go back in.

And we waited and waited.

Eventually, I went back round the corner to find out what the delay was, only to discover that all the other groups had gone back into the building. They had neglected to tell us it was safe to return. To top it all off, they had locked the back gate and we were forced to walk a much longer route round all the houses to be able to get to the front entrance. Needless to say, we were most upset and expressed that in a suitably British way which involved much muttering under our breath.

PART 4

A day in the life of a tutor:

Dealing with "naughty" students

LATE COMERS

And so, it came to pass that students didst neglect to leave enough time to travel and so camest unto the tutorial late.

And the tutor didst look at them most severely.

And they didst wither inside with guilt and blurt out an apology for they were British and much grovelling was to be had....

Chapter 2 verse 13 of the sacred book of tutorials.

Alas, it is sad to say that some students just don't have the respect that is appropriate for the sacred tutorial. When it becomes clear to me that at least one student will be late, I ensure that I instruct the students who have already arrived in how they should act when the latecomer finally arrives.

They should look at their watches and simultaneously take a sharp corporate intake of breath. When student is particularly late, I ask the rest of the group to perform the ancient British technique of disapproval; tutting. A good tutting helps set the right tone for future tutorials.

However, in recent years I have realised that it's not environmentally friendly to throw away that guilt latecomers feel just after one use. Instead I reuse it in a way that it helps others too. And by others, I mean me.

Now when a student comes in late and says, "I'm sorry," I reply, "that's okay, I like chocolate."

Most are too flustered at that point to take much in, but occasionally one looks at me as if to ask, "Is he serious?"

No, I'm not serious, I'm John *dad joke level up* but I do want some chocolate.

THE STUDENT WHO WAS ALWAYS LATE

Unfortunately, there's always one student for whom the whole guilt thing goes over their head.

One particular student had been late by about 20 minutes for the first two of my 101/CT3/CS1 tutorials. Heck, he was even late back from lunch.

Naturally, he being a Brit, we expected him to be profusely apologetic. Sadly, he was completely unperturbed by his wicked time-keeping ways. Talk about taking the biscuit; he was taking the whole packet!

The actuarial code doesn't seem to cover this sort of behaviour, so it was up to me to help him understand the error of his ways.

At the start of the third tutorial, when he again had not yet arrived, I said to the other students, "I want you to go along with me when I put something on the board by saying, 'Yes that's fine.'"

When the student eventually did arrive, I flipped my computer to a different screen which was full of equations from the more demanding 106/CT6/CS2.

The errant student sat down and furiously copied the equations from the board whilst I added a bit of explanation and then said to the class, "Okay, so is that all clear?"

"Yes!" the other students all chorused.

"All right then, let's move on." I announced.

And with that, I flipped the screen back to the actual 101/CT3/CS1 tutorial notes and continued.

Sadly, my memory is such that I can't remember if I let him on the joke, but I'd like to think that he laughed and learnt an important lesson.

THE STUDENT WHO CAME TO THE WRONG TUTORIAL

So I was teaching statistics in London and a student arrived 10 minutes late terribly flustered and apologetic. I was already in full swing teaching so I didn't bother to check the register at that moment but just carried on.

Now usually late arriving students become less flustered over time, but this particular student seemed to get more and more agitated the longer he stayed until after about 10 minutes he nervously raised a hand and asked, "Excuse me, is this accounting?"

"No, this is actuarial statistics," I replied in a superior tone.

The relief on his face was tangible as he realised he was in the wrong room and wouldn't have to understand what on earth we were doing.

"Oh thank you so much!"

I've never seen someone pack up and exit the room so fast, except perhaps when teaching 301/CA1/CP1.

For the record, it should be noted the extreme level of

restraint I exercised by not replying, "You're out of your depth boy!" as I think at that moment he was already fully cognisant of the difference between actuarial and accounting exams.

MOBILE PHONES

Back when I started tutoring, students only had Nokia bricks or Blackberries. Texting took too long and as actuaries never actually want to phone people, there was little temptation to become distracted. But things have changed and some students seem to think that fiddling on their phone instead of listening to me is acceptable. As I feel it's important to my ego, I correct them in this matter.

It amuses me that some students try to hide what they're doing by using their phone under the table, forgetting that I can actually see them as the tables have no sides. But it's nothing that a little teasing at their expense can't fix. The following exchange usually does the job:

"I hate to think what you're doing with your hands down there in your lap..."

The student looks up in horror, "I was just using my phone." They quickly wave the phone to demonstrate the veracity of their statement.

"A likely tale," I reply before moving on.

Over time, students have become more blatant about their

phone use, leaving it on their desk and replying to incoming messages. My method of shaming needed to be upgraded in order to respond to the times. My usual approach is something like this:

"How insensitive can you be? Showing off to us all that you actually have friends?! Think of the pain you're causing those actuarial students around you!"

Sometimes students point out that it isn't friends distracting them but their need to have constant updates on the cricket score. I must admit, this is a suitable British thing to do. Nevertheless, they are clearly being selfish by not updating the whole class on how much our great country is losing by.

I think my lowest point concerning phones was when one student, who sat at the front, scrolled through T-shirts on a shopping website while I was teaching. I mean, it's just downright depressing that a bit of fabric is considered more interesting than my explanation of moment generating functions.

TALKING IN CLASS

This isn't a problem that I, as an actuarial tutor, face. Personally, I like a bit of banter in class. Otherwise, I might as well be delivering a lecture at college or a DJ on an online LIVE tutorial.

The real issue here, as you have and will continue to see, is getting students *to* talk. Fortunately, my subject is statistics which doesn't require discussion or working as a group to find an answer. Well, unless you include those pairs of students who say they are working together. This invariably means one is working and the other is providing encouragement by copying down all their answers.

THE QUIETEST CLASS EVER

I once taught a class that so quiet it was painful. After an explanation, I'd ask if everything was okay. Nothing. I was left wondering what the silence meant. Were they are confused and didn't know what on earth was going on? Or were they bored out of their large minds? For groups such as these, I created large thumbs that students can hold up or down to indicate their level of happiness:

Think of these thumbs as the actuarial equivalent of Caesar at the Imperial Games, with the students' minds as gladiators and my teaching as the wild beasts.

Yeah, I know they're just boring laminated paper thumbs, but an actuary can dream. Usually in shades of grey and about fixing that Excel macro, but we can still dream.

After years of not *quite* needing to use them I eventually filed them somewhere in my study and forgot about them until this day. As such, there was no non-verbal method available to me to discern what they were thinking. Twenty years of marriage had clearly demonstrated that my mind reading skills were unreliable at best.

Based on their lack of response as to how students are doing, I tend to use a minimax solution and assume that students are struggling to understand. I try to minimise this event by going slower and giving more careful explanation. So gradually this particular tutorial got slower and slower.

I told jokes, but there was no response. Not even a groan or a whimper. Nothing. At. All. I began to grow self-conscious about my humour. My delivery became more and more awkward until eventually I stopped with the whole humour thing and I just gave them a generic tutorial.

I'd ask questions about the tutorial work. Nothing. At. All. Their individual work on questions seemed fine as I went around the class and checked. I began to feel paranoid. Why wouldn't they answer any questions I asked them?

Eventually it became just too much. I threw down the gauntlet to the class, asking yet another question then challenging them with: "I'm not going to move on until I get an answer."

Though I can't remember the question, I do remember the silence.

Forget getting blood out of a stone, it was like performing open heart surgery on a concrete block.

I had backed myself into a corner. I couldn't go back unless I lost face and accepted that the students would say nothing for the remainder of the tutorials.

And so I kept waiting.

And waiting.

And waiting.

It felt like hours, but it was probably only about 30 minutes[18].

---

[18] Okay, I'm exaggerating. Probably more like 5 minutes of utter silence. If you're a Millennial or Gen Z then just imagine no internet for 2 minutes and you'll understand.

Until eventually one of them laughed at how silly it was and answered the question.

The tension had been broken. The point was made.

In some ways they still won because I realised that if it took this long to answer one simple question then asking any more that day would mean that we'd be lucky to make it halfway through the first chapter by the end of the tutorial. I had to pull up my big boy pants and accept that the rest of this tutorial would just be a dull lecture.

I still get palpitations now thinking about it.

FORGETTING EQUIPMENT

The most common misdemeanours amongst actuarial students is, without a doubt, turning up without the full complement of equipment. You'd think that students who achieved exceptional results at A level and university, and who so impressed the recruiters that they were admitted into one of the most demanding professions in the world, would have the acumen to realise that they would need a writing implement. It never dawned on them that they would also need something to use said writing implement upon, as well as a calculator and their copy of the sacred actuarial tables. Blessed be their name.

However, it's quite common that a few students to think that they alone amongst all other students can survive the perils of a statistics tutorial without one or more of these four basic tools. I think it must be some kind of rite of passage in order to be accepted amongst the ranks of the student heroes that have gone before and whose deeds are sung aloud to keep one's spirits up when performing pension valuations.

Some of these students soldier on, using abandoned pens, scribbling on corners of the question handout, using their phone as a calculator, and searching online for statistical tables to calculate probabilities. But others quickly realise the

Herculean task set before them and look like lost puppies. As I'm more of a cat person, I easily resist the power of the puppy eyes.

As a tutor, I have to choose between one of the following three responses:

1. I bail them out and lend them what is lacking in their equipment department. But by doing so, I am then introducing moral hazard for future tutorials. Though perhaps this could be mitigated by reminding them that I like chocolate on the off-chance that my generosity might be repaid in the universal currency of the humble cocoa bean.

2. I can let them suffer, knowing that without such tools they will achieve little beyond learning an important lesson about preparation – which is bound to be helpful in future life. Well, at least in the upcoming examinations.

3. I could use this moment to encourage them to seek help from their fellow students on the off-chance that this will spark a lasting friendship born out of their equipment tragedy. Maybe in years to come some qualified actuary on their wedding day will say, "If it hadn't been for John

suggesting that I talked to the person next to me then this would have never been..."

By using my Capital Project Appraisal techniques, I have found that I can maximise the net present value of chocolate by a combination of options 1 and 2: Make them suffer for a bit and then lend my equipment and remind them frequently of my love of chocolate.

Back when I was a secondary school teacher, you'd only lend students equipment in return for one of their shoes. As no student would walk out of the classroom with only one shoe, no student would walk out the classroom with my equipment. But fine upstanding mature actuarial students surely didn't need such methods employed to ensure I get my equipment back. What could possibly go wrong?

Suffice to say that one student took my sacred copy of the actuarial tables on our last tutorial together. And despite my emailing them, they did not respond nor return them through the post. The police didn't seem to take this crime seriously when I reported it. My local MP did not feel that introducing stricter laws covering the theft of actuarial tables was worthy of his consideration.

This must be how it feels for someone's spouse to run off with someone else. I couldn't believe my tables would have left me like that. Unless my tables weren't a willing participant in their elopement and were actually kidnapped! But I have to say that it was shoddy kidnapping as I never even received a ransom note.

That's probably why I like going to Paddington station as they have signs warning, "Professional pickpockets operate in this area." It's such a relief to know that if you're going to be pickpocketed, it will be done by a professional and not some second-rate criminal.

I wonder if the thieving profession has qualifications so that only those who pass are entitled to call themselves professional pickpockets? And are they regulated?

Anyway, I digress.

It goes without saying that I had difficulty getting to sleep without my actuarial tables to comfort me through the night. I had to undergo grief counselling before I was able to let them go. Some insensitive colleagues told me that there were plenty more actuarial tables in the Profession's online shop, but I knew none of them would be the same as my beloved Tina the Tables.

SETTING THE EXAMPLE

Fortunately, as a qualified member of the actuarial profession, I never forget things. Oh no. But if, hypothetically (ahem), I had, then I would definitely claim it to be the fault of my age, rather than disorganisation. The worst thing about growing old is issues with memory which can cause me to lose track of what I'm doing, because the worst thing about growing older is issues with memory which can cause me to lose track of what I'm doing.

THE TUTORIAL WHERE I WORE DARK GLASSES

I'm rather short-sighted. Probably something to do with staring at spreadsheets too long, I suspect. Remember this and remember I've previously mentioned how I travel to the train station on my motorbike.

It would make sense that to put on my "motorbike" helmet I would need to take off my glasses. On one occasion, for some reason, I decided to do this outside rather than in the usual confined space of our utility room. I placed my glasses on top of the rubbish wheelie bin[19] for safe keeping. However, as happens when you have OCD, I noticed a piece of rubbish in the garden that I decided to put in said wheelie bin that very instant before putting my glasses back on, which meant I needed to lift up the lid to place the rubbish in the bin. And bizarrely, even with all my education, I was surprised to find that my glasses were no longer on said bin lid when I resumed the task of placing my helmet on.

As any of you who are short-sighted can sympathise, trying to

---

[19] Just to clarify: that's a wheelie bin for rubbish rather than a rubbish (ie useless) wheelie bin.

find your glasses when you're short-sighted is not easy. Particularly if it's in the semi-darkness of an autumn morning at 6.25am. As much as I tried, I just couldn't find them. I was forced to leave without them in order to catch my train. The only prescription glasses I had that day were my sunglasses.

If you saw me sitting on the train or travelling on the tube wearing my dark glasses you may have mistaken me for being cool. I can assure you that I felt anything but.

Even worse, I had to wear them during the tutorial if I were to see anything other than a pink blob for people's faces. More importantly, I needed to see the students' work so I could mark it. Embarrassed doesn't begin to describe how I felt.

I rushed home afterwards hoping I would be able to locate them, only to discover that my children had picked them up, wondering why Daddy would leave them right in the middle of the path. *sigh*

PART 5

A day in the life of a tutor:

Teaching students

ENCOURAGING STUDENTS TO ANSWER QUESTIONS

So, let's get to the heart of the tutorial – teaching students. Writing stuff on a board and getting students to copy it is called lecturing. This has been shown to be one of the most ineffective forms of learning. However, it can be very effective in sending students to sleep. Student actuaries who work in pensions are the exception, as the daily exposure to monotony has built up their immunity to such an extent that they resist all lesser forms of tedium such as lecturing.

I do try to make tutorials as interactive as possible by asking students questions and encouraging them to ask questions in return. However, as you've already seen, resilient student actuaries are quite apt in resisting my attempts to question them. I do my best by trying various techniques to reduce the fear of getting the wrong answer. Wrong answers are mere stepping stones to learning and arriving at the right answer.

One technique I employ is to encourage students to try again if they get it wrong. For example, I might ask "If 'n' increases, will the credibility factor increase or decrease?"

"Increase," says one student.

"Almost," I reply encouragingly, "try again."

"Decrease," they answer.

"See, I knew you'd get it," I respond enthusiastically.

Sometimes the issue at hand is the fear of getting it wrong in front of other students. I try to dismantle that fear by saying, "You're amongst friends or at least people that you'll never meet again."

At other times, when a student answers a question wrong, the rest of the group suddenly knows the right answer and all will volunteer. I try to encourage that first student by saying how grateful the rest of the group was for the first student who "took one for the team" so the group could step over that student's dead body and give the right answer. What teamwork!

When there is a common error that I know many students make, I deliberately make that mistake in my calculations on the board and get the students to tell me what I've done wrong. It's always easier to point out someone else's mistakes than spot your own. There have been occasions when the mistakes I made may not be deliberate. Ahem. At such times, when they pointed out my error, I admitted, "When we began

JOHN LEE | 113

this tutorial, I was the master and you were the padawan[20].

Now *you* are the master."

---

[20] For those of you that haven't watched any Star Wars films, a *padawan* is a Jedi apprentice. Of course, if you've not watched the series, you'll have no idea about what a Jedi is either. Just imagine I'm addressing you as a young learner and you'll be fine. Okay, carry on.

GETTING STUDENTS TO ASK QUESTIONS

If prodding students to answer questions is challenging, then getting them to ask me questions is even harder. Most of my students are postgraduates. This means I have to undo the damage university education has caused. These beloved institutions are paid for bums on seats and research. The former requires good advertising or a good reputation. The latter requires clever academics who are unlikely to be able to communicate for toffee[21] and hence struggle to explain things to lowly underclasses.

Having attended Oxford University, I've experienced this first hand. When I didn't understand something, I asked my tutor for help, to which he replied, "It's obvious."

I responded, "If it were obvious then I wouldn't be asking."

The tutor looked baffled and attempted to explain. This only served to make me even more confused than before as they continued to illustrate their inability to explain concepts to people whose brains didn't ooze out of their ears. I can't think

---

[21] Though maybe for liquorice.

what inspired me to enter teaching.

As a slight aside, one of my maths tutor's jokes amply demonstrates the different world that he operated in:

"Choose a number between one and ten."

"7," I replied.

"Ha, it's rational," he laughed.

Me: *confused look*

"There's infinitely more irrational numbers than rational numbers so it's irrational that you chose a rational one," he explained.

Me: *even more confused look*

The only thing I learnt from his joke was to choose the number root pi whenever somebody asks me to choose a number between one and ten.

Now since university lecturers are hired to research to get grants, lecturing is often the least important part of their job, except perhaps as an opportunity to stoke their ego by demonstrating how clever they are. And so, they've developed a way of making students feel incredibly stupid for asking questions.

This leads these students to say in my tutorials, "Sorry to ask, but..."

How am I supposed to respond to this?

"Yes, how dare you come to a tutorial not knowing everything and then have the audacity to ask me a question?!"

Or one of my students might say, "Sorry if this is a stupid question, but..."

To which I interrupt and ask, "Do you know the answer?" They reply, "No." So I add, "Well then, it's not a stupid question."

THE STUDENT WHO SAID "AH!"

I had one student who I thought was really knowledgeable of the course as he both answered the majority of my questions and did well when answering exam questions. However, despite his apparent knowledge, whenever I was explaining something, he kept saying "Ah!" as if he suddenly understood something that was previously unclear.

I couldn't reconcile how he seemed to have excellent understanding and yet still be saying "Ah!"

When I enquired, I discovered that he hadn't actually read the notes for the course at all. Instead he had learnt everything from the summary flashcards. Apparently, he knew *what* to do, but he had no idea exactly *why* he was doing it.

Wonders to self if this story is an allegory of a lot of an actuaries' lives in the office...

PEDAGOGY

Such a cool word, eh? Shame I can't pronounce it, which ruins the effect of using such a prestigious word to impress people. But let's ignore that and briefly mention other techniques I use to help students in tutorials.

Strengthening their neural pathways

By getting students to *recall* information, they re-fire the neural pathway in their brain that stores that piece of information, which then strengthens that connection and makes it easier for them to remember that information in the future. So I repeatedly ask them to recall the same fact throughout the day, for example the definition of an MGF, until they all chant the correct answer in unison. In other circles, this technique is known as brainwashing and is successfully used in a variety of military purposes.

Resist spoon-feeding them

When a student makes a mistake, I often circle the error in their work, and then move on without explanation. I don't do this to be annoying, although it is a bonus side-effect of this teaching technique, but so that they have the opportunity to figure it out for themselves. I studied it as part of my M. Ed. Honest! I mean would I lie to you[22]?

Friendly competition

One way to spur students on to develop a dull but necessary skill, such as looking up results in the tables, is to use a bit of friendly competition. "Find the page in your tables which has the formula for the normal normal posterior. Last one there's an accountant!"

Comparing methods to find the best

I first show them the hard way of doing something, like finding the log-likelihood for a generalised linear model, and then I show them a cunning shortcut that gets the same answer in a fraction of the time, like expressing the original PDF as a power of an exponential.

Oh alright, I confess. That's not to help them learn but for them to appreciate how fantastic my cunning shortcut is on the off chance that they burst into spontaneous applause and throw money or chocolate.

---

[22] Frequently, as this book clearly demonstrates, but let's not get hung up on that.

Showing how things work in real life

I know it's bizarre to even consider that something student actuaries learn for their exams actually has a real-life application, but accidents do happen. For example, if I wanted to explain how a death-in-service benefit works, I get one of the students to put me down as their beneficiary and then arrange for an accident. This method of teaching has the bonus effect of supplementing my tutor income.

If you are concerned about my methodology being unethical and would rather that I supplemented my income in other ways, then please feel free to buy more copies of this book for your actuarial colleagues or contribute to my Go Fund Me page.

Using banter

Rather than to just offer a generic tutorial, I like to throw a little personal teasing into the mix. However, since some actuarial students don't appear to have a sense of humour, this can backfire. For example, I joked in a CT6 tutorial about how students who receive a CT3 exemption tend to fail CT6. To which one student retorted, "I'll have you know that I worked hard for my exemption!" I was taken aback as I said it tongue-in-cheek teasing around and wasn't serious, although the empirical evidence supported my joke. I soon realised it was probably better to apologise than to defend my banter. Although, according to the IFoA's Code of Conduct, swords at dawn is an honourable way to settle such arguments.

Topical jokes

To show my versatility, I tell jokes that are specific to the topic I'm teaching.

For example, when summing a geometric series to obtain the MGFs of a discrete distribution, the following joke is appropriate:

A mathematician walks into a bar and asks for a pint. A second mathematician walks in and asks for half a pint. A third mathematician asks for a quarter of a pint. And so on. The bartender takes one look at the infinite queue of mathematicians and sighs, "You mathematicians should really know your limits!" and pours them two pints.

When teaching the various formulae for finding the present value of annuities, I can use:

An actuary walks into a bar, where a bar is an annuity paid continuously.

Or when looking at credibility estimates we talk about how the prior becomes more reliable as its variance decreases, until the extreme case where the variance is zero, *ie* the prior is saying it is this single number. Which leads on to the ultimate statistical put-down:

Your mother's so mean she has no variance.

Or when looking at the linear regression model $y_i = \alpha + \beta x_i$ I point out that the x_i is the explanatory variable and the y_i is the northern variable. To which they all look confused until I say, "why aye". Admittedly, some still look confused. Probably because they're southerners and have never heard northerners speak.

And finally, who can forget to point out how the form of the exponential family

$$f(y) = \exp\left\{\frac{y\theta - b(\theta)}{a(\phi)} + c(y, \phi)\right\}$$

helps statisticians connect to the internet, as c is a function of y ϕ.

On occasion, groups laugh way more than my jokes deserve, which is pretty much any laughter at all. This makes me a little nervous as I had a rather unfortunate incident many years ago as a teacher that left a permanent scar on my psyche.

It was a Year 8 maths lesson I thought was going rather well. They were laughing at my jokes and there was a "buzz" about the whole lesson. However, a niggling thought at the back of my mind kept saying "John, you're not *that* funny." My ego brushed it off and I carried on regardless. As the end of the lesson drew to a close, one of the students approached me, saying, "Sir, prepare to be embarrassed...we see your underpants."

I looked down and it was true. Back then, I tucked my shirt into my underpants. On that particular day, the shirt had pulled them above my trouser line. The swines didn't bother to tell me for the whole hour.

Let's just say that I have never tucked my shirt into my underpants since.

So now when a group is laughing just a little too much, I quickly check to make sure my flies are done up and nothing else is amiss.

TRAINING UP IN OTHER AREAS

In addition to training actuarial students so they can pass their professional exams, I offer them a little bonus and teach them some transferrable skills.

Particularly, I teach them the importance of stating their assumptions clearly when communicating. This is a key part of our actuarial work. The following examples serve to show how I help them sharpen these thought processes:

"Can I ask a question?"

"You just did."

"Can I ask another?"

"You just did."

Eventually, they realise that they either need to ask for permission to ask two questions or they just need to punch me in the face.

***

"I have a question."

"I have an answer: Thursdays at 4 o'clock."

When they look at me bemused, I add, "I'm guessing that my answer wasn't for your question."

***

A student who missed a bit of my notes on the screen as I scrolled down, asks, "Can you go up?"

I stand on a chair.

***

"Can you help me?" asks a student.

"Yes," I reply whilst remaining where I am.

Student gets upset

AM I BORING YOU?

Quite often when I'm explaining something, a student gets up and walks out the room. Just like that!

Clearly, I've done something wrong. And so, I try and fix it right then and there.

As they step out, I shout, "Give me another chance! I'll try harder! I'll even stop telling these awful jokes!" I confess, I might have my fingers crossed behind my back as I say that last bit.

To which they respond rather sheepishly[23], "I'm just going to the loo."

I can see why they didn't want to say anything as they left the room in the first place. Announcing they were going to the loo in front of 12 other people would have been quite embarrassing.

Well I'm glad I was sensitive enough to save them from all that.

---

[23] I wonder if sheep can look sheep-ish. And if they do does that mean that they are only part sheep and not exactly a sheep?

At times, students surprise me with their candour, announcing to me and the class that they are just nipping to the toilet. The foot's really on the other hand now as I feel rather awkward knowing that level of detail. To cover my awkwardness, I embrace their openness by asking, "Number 1 or number 2?"

GOING AROUND AND HELPING STUDENTS

A key part of a tutorial involves setting the students exam questions from the question handout and then going around the classroom and giving individual feedback. This is the only way to see how much the students understand.

Well I suppose it's not the *only* way. I suspect some torture techniques could also extract that information. But such barbaric approaches are not considered orthodox in actuarial circles. That being said, pension valuations waver particularly close to the line.

THE STUDENT WHO WANTED THE SOLUTIONS

I had just given the class the first question of the day from the tutorial handout, when a student asked, "Can I have the solutions?"

I was a bit taken aback and asked, "Why?"

"Well, I find it much easier with the solutions," she replied.

"I'm sure you do, but you don't receive the solutions in the exam. I suggest that it's a good idea to practise without." I explained.

She got very upset by this and wouldn't be placated.

Sadly she failed the exam, presumably because those invigilators were as inflexible as me about the whole solutions thing. We are clearly terrible people.

TICKS

For this section, my American readers need to recall that ticks are what we British call checkmarks[24]. Otherwise you're going to be somewhat confused about my so-called method of encouragement.

One way of encouraging students is to put ticks on their work. Everyone loves ticks, well except perhaps for dogs[25], as they give you that warm glowy feeling inside. Rather like eating barium.

However, there was the time that I put an encouraging tick on a young lady's work only to have her recoil in horror. "How dare you write on my work!" I was taken aback. It appeared that the encouragement was outweighed by the fact that my tick had 'ruined' her beautiful working.

Thereafter, whenever I came near to check her work, she would hold it carefully out of arms reach to prevent my red pen coming anywhere near it.

---

[24] Honestly, I don't know why I bothered with the UK-US glossary at the beginning if I then repeat myself throughout.

[25] British students will find this play on the word 'tick' funny. My apologies for Americans that are still getting used to the idea of ticks being something nice.

Over years of teaching students, I came to realise that this was just one expression of the OCD behaviour often exhibited by actuaries. A fun way to stir the OCD pot is to switch the order of the dx and dy when teaching calculating double integrals of joint distributions:

$$\int_{x=0}^{1} \int_{y=0}^{1} \frac{2}{5}(3x+2y)\, dx\, dy$$

"They need to be nested!" they cry out in anguish.

Another notable example was a student who arranged the writing implements on her desk in a very particular way. If one of the pens got knocked ever so slightly, she would have to straighten it before she was able to continue.

In retrospect, I think my turning one of her items 15 degrees while she went to use the loo was perhaps a tad childish.

Another group of students who don't take kindly to me placing ticks on their work are those who use an electronic tablet instead of paper. I'm not really sure what it is about using a permanent marker on their tablet's screen that causes them such distress, but I'm sure I'll figure it out one of these days.

Occasionally, students do something a little bit special and ticks are not sufficient to express my delight. I need to use something like a gold sticky star. Given that most of my students are aged 22-30, perhaps I should use something more mature and professional: the smiley face.

Rewarding students with these leads to much jealousy from their peers. Who knew that smiley faces were in such demand? But I can't just give them out to everyone as that would devalue the whole smiley face currency leading to a collapse of the positive emoticon economy. Though I suppose there could be the option of creating a higher value smiley face: a smiley face with hair...

THE INJUSTICES OF NO WORKING

One of the frustrations of making the rounds and checking answers, finding errors, and giving helpful pointers is finding students who don't show their calculations. As an examiner, we call this "answer roulette". Get it right and they win. Get it wrong and they lose everything.

As a tutor, I duly urge students to show their calculations so they reduce the chances of making mistakes. Showing their work increases the number of marks they will be awarded in the exam should they make a mistake[26]. Now whilst many students listen to their wise tutor and take heed of his sage counsel, some students persist in their evil no-working ways. Some soon receive their comeuppance when they make a mistake due to skipping one too many steps. As their beloved tutor, I can then use the time-honoured phrase of "I told you so" to encourage them to learn from their error of their ways.

However, a persistent minority continue without showing

---

[26] For there's none of those multi-choice questions in our rock solid British actuarial exams. Well apart from the business and economic exams but they don't count.

their calculations and continue to get the right answer. It's just not the way the world should be. I ask these students if they could be so kind as to make a mistake so that they learn the right lesson and set a good example to the class. But still some resist and still get the correct answer. There's simply no justice and so I have to take the law into my own hands and mark their correct answer wrong.

DIVERSITY

Diversity is a big issue for some people these days, well except when it comes to diversity of thought – but that's a whole other can of worms. So I try to embrace multiculturalism by encouraging my students, using a variety of languages and dialects.

However, whilst I may be good at maths, my skills at languages are somewhat limited. What I lack in knowledge, I make up for in enthusiasm and imagination. Since the actuarial profession attracts students from all over the world, it was only a matter of time before my bluffing became exposed for the façade that it is. For example, in one tutorial, I was instructing students in my faux French to get their *calculateurs*, only to have a French student laugh out loud before telling me that it's actually *calculatrice*.

Another rather unexpected faux pas was the chi squared distribution. I pronounce it "k-eye" like many mathematicians, though I have heard some pronounce it "ch-eye". However, we all stood corrected by a Greek student who asked, "Why you say k-eye when it's ch-ee?"

Well now I is real educated but trying to change my

pronunciation after 30 years of use has proved to be a Herculean task. Even if I were successful in pronouncing chi properly, I would then have my non-Greek students confused by my correct pronunciation.

Now sadly we mathematicians are considered particularly un-woke by progressives as we are bigoted enough to suggest that questions only have one right answer. This seems to be particularly offensive to those who struggle at maths and want their different answer to be accepted.

Whilst I try to be encouraging, it's vital that I tell students the truth. For example, "Your integration sucks." Actually, this is so true of math grads. Perhaps they spent so long doing advanced maths, they've forgotten the basics like integration by parts. In fact, I once had a tutorial with ten maths graduates and two students that had joined the Profession straight after A levels. The A level students were absolutely whipping the graduates at integration[27].

Occasionally, I like to mix things up a bit by ticking wrong answers or correcting answers before I realise they're actually

---

[27] I should point out that "whipping" does not mean A level students were literally whipping the others. It's slang for beating the other students. Oh wait, no really that's not literal beating either. I mean they were thrashing. Oh no. I give up. Just call the police now.

already correct. I then have to correct my correcting by crossing it out with more red ink. Students at times become concerned over my inability to tell the right answer from the wrong answer, which I blame on the diversity training I've received. I tell them not to worry, as I am an examiner. I feel that this gives students great confidence that I know what I'm doing and also assure them of the robustness of the exam system.

MAKING STUDENTS NERVOUS

Now despite my encouragement and friendly demeanour, I've noticed I still make students nervous when I stand near them. One of the heart-breaking things for me as a tutor is seeing student's hands shake when I'm looking at their work. Sometimes, they even shake when I'm not looking at them at all. Though how I'd know their hands were shaking when I'm not looking at them is a flaw in my assertion.

Admittedly, as I pause when going around the room, there can be that sense of impending doom. Perhaps they believe I'm just about to point out that everything in their answer that they have built their life on is just about to come tumbling down around them. Perhaps they fear if that is the case, they'll need extensive counselling before they can even face starting again. But sometimes I'm just pausing because it takes me a while to read their working or I can see they're just about to finish a question. In all likelihood, I'm waiting for their moment of triumph so I can reward them with a tick or smiley face.

I first noticed the nervous effect I had on students when I was invigilating exams as a secondary school teacher. Wherever I stood in the exam hall, I would always be standing near a student who would then become nervous, thinking I was standing there because of something they'd done. Whereas the reality was that the hall was crammed full of students at examination desks and there was nowhere I could stand that wasn't near someone.

Well...that's not entirely true.

If you think writing exams is boring then you should try invigilating them. It's on a totally different plane of mind crushing dullness. In desperation, we invigilators have to do something to pass the time and liven things up– like play invigilator games.

One invigilator will pose a question amongst the other invigilators, such as, "Who has the worst haircut?" or "Who is most likely to fail?" and then all the invigilators go and stand by the student who garners their vote.

If we get bored of that game, we play Pac Man amongst the desks.

DIRECTION OF TRAVEL

For some reason whenever I circle round the U-shape of desks to help students I always travel in an anti-clockwise direction. After a quick poll amongst my peers, it appears that I am alone amongst the tutors in doing so. Clearly, I've been conditioned by trips to ice-skating rinks which in the UK always go anti-clockwise[28]. In fact, I would probably fall over if anyone asked me to skate the other way.

One consequence of going around and helping students in the same direction; it creates a sporting venue 'Wave' effect[29], but with knowledge. I give a student some help and then coincidentally the next student round just happens to have made progress on that very same issue using the very method I had been explaining to the student before.

Hence, it appears to me that the students sitting on the left-hand side of the U shape are cleverer than those on the right. They always appear to be further on by the time I get to them and have overcome the issues that I had to explain to the students on the right.

---

[28] Rumour is that ice rinks in the southern hemisphere all go the other way.

[29] We Brits call this a Mexican wave as it was first seen by us in the Football (Soccer) World Cup in Mexico 1986.

ACTUARIAL TUTOR SUPERPOWERS

Years of helping students from the inside of desks arranged in a U-shape has meant that I have perfected my ability to read and write upside down. But sadly, my students are not particularly impressed by this skill. Clearly, years of DC and Marvel movies conditioning students have made such actuarial tutor skills dull in comparison. Actually, I suspect that watching grass grow is marginally more interesting than actuaries.

There was the one time when my desk rose mysteriously as I was writing on my laptop. Sadly, this turned out not to be a superpower after all; my super muffin-top belly pressed the button that raises and lowers the desk.

But I do have one superpower that *is* recognised by students as being uncanny.

Students often get the wrong answer on their calculator and call me over for some help but as they recalculate it when I'm standing beside them, they get the right answer, even if previous recalculations without me were wrong.

Now, this has happened so many times that the data suggests that there is a correlation between my standing near them and them getting the right answer.

The only reason for this, however improbable it might seem, is that my presence is somehow having a mystical influence over their calculators.

Without doubt it is my tutor superpower.

When I notice students struggling, I now offer my standing-by-them services so that their calculations go well.

I'm also available for hire in exams to stand near their desk, for very reasonable rates.

PART 6

A day in the life of a tutor:

Taking breaks

BREAKTIMES

Breaktimes for actuarial students are like an oasis in the desert that is full of piranha fish. On the one hand, there is the caffeine that they are craving in the form of coffee, tea, and intravenous drips along with a multitude of biscuits. On the other hand, there is the dread of unstructured time where they might have to engage in small talk.

Some students decide that the opportunity outweighs the potential risks and seize the moment. Though no moment has been more seized than one student whose first three questions of the day were, "What time is break?" followed by, "When's lunch?" and finally, "When do we finish?"

I tell you it really made me feel like they were there to give me their all to my tutorial.

weeps silently

At break, most students amble over to the table where the refreshments await. Some students pretend they are finishing off a question to minimise the amount of time they have to interact with other students. But it's always difficult for them to time this correctly. Spend too short on the question and they'll end up chatting to someone, spend too long and all the best biscuits will have long gone. The cleverer students opt for spending just a little while on a question before grabbing a biscuit before heading straight to the loo without stopping at go, collecting £200, nor engaging in any conversation whatsoever. Winner winner chicken dinner.

The majority of students then return immediately to their seats and look for something to occupy themselves until break is over. Typically, that something is their phone. However, being actuaries, they soon find they have no friends on social media. Scrolling through posts from celebrities only serves to remind them of the dreariness of their life. And so, they end up looking at work emails whilst pretending they're on social media so as to impress their fellow students.

Special shout out to those students from Towers Perrin whom I teased about looking at their work emails, to find out that they were doing exactly that. But they were doing so to see if they'd got an email informing them that they still had their job. This was one of those moments where what started with a little teasing ended up in a very different place to what I'd anticipated.

During the afternoon break, not even a defibrillator and caffeine injected straight into the bloodstream can revive the students enough to get them to engage in conversation. So, I typically resort to putting memes on the board, such as the following:

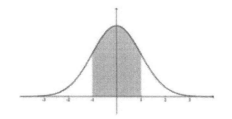

NORMAL DISTRIBUTION

PARANORMAL DISTRIBUTION

$$\frac{\sin(\text{gerine})}{\cos(\text{gerine})} =$$

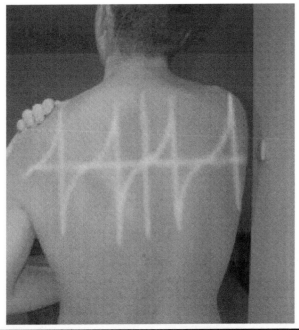

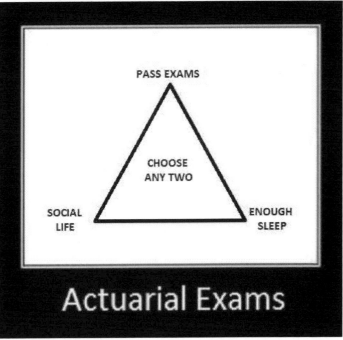

I used to post these on my company's social media channels on Fridays to bolster students before they began their weekend of study. I can't understand why I got taken off that position.

The missing memes

Before I move on, I'd like to take a brief moment to remember those memes that are no longer with us here in this book.

Boromir the Actuary meme: *"One does not simply explain what I do."* A flat refusal from Warner Brothers.

Napoleon Dynamite (aka nerd actuary) meme: *"She showed me her spreadsheet so I guess you could say things are getting pretty serious."* Sadly Fox charges $500-$2,500 per movie still.

The Love Actually film poster Photoshopped to *"Love Actuary: The Ultimate Spreadsheet Comedy."* No reply from Universal Studios.

Though we miss them dearly, their memory will still live on in our hearts...and also in my Twitter feed (ahem):

https://twitter.com/Actuarial_Tutor

BISCUITS

If you were using a GLM to predict the level of student satisfaction, you might consider using covariates such as quality of teaching, improvement in understanding, or the number of questions answered by the tutor. All the factors appear on the feedback forms we ask our students to fill out. However, using the principle of parsimony, I have found that a single factor model containing only the quality of biscuits proved to be 60% more effective.

In short, students think with their stomachs. If you give them doughnuts, then it doesn't matter how you teach. It's probably the reason why trustee meetings have gotten away with their boredom for so long.

Back in the day, some venues only supplied coffee from free coffee machines. And there was a reason why they were free. Coffee was a rather generous name given to what came out of the machines.

But they also had chocomilk and soup flavoured soup, I kid you not! Somehow, I found water, salt, and monosodium glutamate to be a tasty treat.

Nowadays we've moved up market. We have someone

delivering tea, coffee, and biscuits to our room as good biscuits create happy students and happy students give good feedback, I mean do well in their exams.

Through extensive testing, it has been shown that the most desirable biscuit is the bourbon, followed by the custard cream, the fruity shortcake, the digestive, and lastly, the humble ginger biscuit.

As their beloved tutor, it is my sacred duty to fight for the best biscuits I can for me, I mean them.

Firstly, this involves befriending the catering team and thanking them for their hard work. On occasion, this in itself is enough for the team to be more generous when issuing biscuits. Sometimes, I need to ask politely for a few more biscuits or do that British passive-aggressive bantering about something that we're actually serious about. For example, "My students were wondering how much they'd need to pay you to get the really nice biscuits." And when all else fails, I resort to begging.

But when even begging fails, I turn to more advanced techniques.

In many venues, the biscuits are carefully allotted for both the morning and the afternoon breaks by the number of students present. Hoping to confuse the head count, I encourage the students to move around the room and thus distract the catering team, leading to extra biscuits. I hide the untouched "rubbish biscuits" after morning break in the hopes of obtaining a full new complement of fresh biscuits in the afternoon[30].

However, one venue has a pile of biscuits, which is restocked daily for the various tutorial groups. However, its apparent generosity sits on a throne of lies. For under the thinnest layer of bourbons and custard creams lies hidden a mound of unwanted digestives and ginger biscuits.

This is the final absorbing state of the Markov biscuit chain process. Students eat the nice biscuits, leaving the rubbish ones. The catering team then add a few more biscuits to the pile for the next tutorial group. Students eat the nice biscuits and leave the rubbish ones and so on.

The growing size of this mountain of unwanted of biscuits then deters the addition of nicer biscuits for future generations of students. And so, as the selfless tutor I am, I sacrifice myself for the betterment of tutorial snacks by taking home

---

[30] Please note that these unloved biscuits are returned to the plate and are not forcibly kept against their will.

those unwanted digestives and ginger nuts, attempting to persuade my children that they are a special treat just for them and not just another freebie from work.

On occasion, due to old age, I forget about the biscuits I take home in my bag. Weeks later, I discover that they'd turned into biscuit dust in the interim. At that point, I take two minutes of silence to remember those that have gone before us. Ashes to ashes, biscuit dust to biscuit dust.

THE STUDENT WHO LEFT

Perhaps one of the most depressing breaktimes for me was when I was teaching a 101/CT3/CS1 tutorial. At morning break a student announced to me he'd decided that he wasn't going to take this subject anymore and promptly packed his bags and left.

Two hours of my quality tuition and this was his conclusion. I mean did he even have enough data to predict what the rest of the day, let alone the subsequent days of tuition, were going to be like?

So, there I was, bereft and heartbroken. The remaining students appeared either shocked or jealous. It was difficult to tell through my tears. Though to be fair, most students are a little shocked the first time I teach them. The fact that tutorials and learning can be fun often causes nausea and palpitations. However, most students safely move through this initial phase into calm acceptance of this strange reality they've entered.

THE BREAKTIME OF HORROR

I arrived at the venue late one day, only to discover that I had not only forgotten the students' name cards but also my laptop. To cap it all off, when the students came in, I discovered that I was teaching a subject I had no knowledge about!

I woke up in a cold sweat, which was disturbing as I went to sleep in a bed.

Enough of this frivolity, however! I want to tell you about the most unusual breaktime I experienced as a tutor. It came from a group that was decidedly un-actuarial. For they not only asked questions and engaged in banter during the tutorial, but horror of horrors, they engaged in uninhibited conversation during the breaktimes!

A student who swapped into the tutorial on the second day was just as bewildered as I was. He sat there at break trying to keep his eyes down on his phone and remain calm. But alas, it was to no avail. If only he had stored a photo of a spreadsheet on his phone for such emergencies.

But what was even more disturbing was their consumption of biscuits at the break. For I found not one, not two but THREE packets of bourbons left when the session resumed.

What kind of depravity is this?

As an upstanding member of the actuarial community there was only one thing I could do: report them to the Profession for their clear breach of the Actuaries Code of Conduct.

I'm pleased to say that the disciplinary board took the matter of their lack of compliance to awkward silences and stilted conversation very seriously indeed. They suggested that these students might be better suited to another profession like well, *you-know-who...*

LUNCHTIMES

If breaktimes are a trial for actuarial students, then lunchtimes are doubly so. Well technically 4.5 times. Breaks are 10 minutes and lunch 45 minutes and 45 minutes are.... hold on, you're probably a mathematician so I don't need to explain that to you.

First of all is their worry of whether they can safely leave their actuarial tables, calculators, and other equipment in the room. Being a kindly tutor, I reassure them I will stay back in the room during lunch break, as I'm 'Billy No Mates'. I also ask if they could leave their valuables on their desks as it saves me having to bend down to root through their bags. I find that sets them at ease.

Joking aside, one of my students actually did have her phone stolen outside a tutorial venue in London. As she stood on the pavement talking on it, someone riding by on a motorbike snatched it right out of her hands. Poor lass, I lent her my Nokia brick phone so she could contact the police and her insurer. She didn't seem impressed by my suggestion that purchasing a phone like mine would prevent future thefts.

But even worse than this was the student who had had their

bag stolen, which contained all his revision notes. He was absolutely distraught as it was only about a month before the exams. It's tragedies like these that remind you of what is really important. BBC revealed how biased its news service is against actuaries by not covering this horrific story during the evening news.

The second worry for students at lunchtime is where and how to obtain food. I send them foraging into the wild streets like some Neanderthal actuary armed with nothing but a slide rule. Despite my encouragement to try something new and different, the fear proves too much. They usually return with a paper sack from McDonalds.

The final worry for students is where should they consume their food. The options are as follows:

Return to the teaching room

Pros: Familiar

Cons: May have to engage in conversation with the tutor and other students.

Cunning solution: Return to the room and wear massive noise cancelling headphones. Keep your eyes fixed on phone screen to successfully convey unavailability.

Eat in the students' common room

Pros: Other amenities might be there, like a bar football table for example.

Cons: Realising you have no friends to play bar football with.

Cunning solution: Invent imaginary friends. You'll have friends and you'll beat them at bar football and feel so much better about your skills.

Eat in the breakout areas outside the teaching room.

Pros: Avoids sitting near the tutor.

Cons: Everyone walking through this area looking at you as you sit on your own, thinking, "Loser."

Cunning solution: Pretend to have Tourette's or some other visible disability. You'll keep the table to yourself and anyone judging you for being on your own will feel guilty.

HOW LONG IS THE PERFECT LUNCHBREAK?

It's a good question. Many years ago, I used to give my students an hour but that meant that that long of a break caused student actuaries to run out of work emails to answer. This would lead to them realising they had no life. Some would become so desperate that they would end up chatting to other students. Few recovered from this bout of socialitus and were often subject to disciplinary procedures and then politely asked to leave the Profession.

As a result, I found 45 minutes works well, except for those students at one venue in London who go to the local pizzeria at lunch. On one hand, I want to congratulate those students for going to a non-standard food venue, on the other hand they are always late back and the carb overload causes them to drift off in the afternoon.

I was once asked by a group if they could reduce their lunchbreak to 30 mins so they could go home 15 minutes early. It seemed a reasonable idea but having seen how shattered they were in the afternoon I've never let another group try it. On second thought, is it fair to make this ruling based on only one data point?

PART 7

A day in the life of a tutor:

The Afternoon of Doom

THE AFTERNOON

As a tutor, I thank the students for coming back after lunch.

Why? Because, not every student does return. I actually did have a student who just disappeared and never returned after the break. Were they abducted? Did they hope I wouldn't tell their employer they had bunked off in the afternoon? The first thing this particular student did upon arrival at the tutorial was to take the notes provided them in advance of the tutorial out of the shrink-wrap, thus indicating that they had not studied them beforehand, hence I suspect the latter to be true.

It's important that I promptly start teaching after lunch break. If you give students an inch, they'll take a mile and you'll end up being 1759 yards, 2 feet, and 11 inches in debt. And so, I begin promptly, even if to a slightly decimated group. My hope being that the other students who return late to the room are shamed enough so that they don't do it again, or better yet, give me chocolate.

It doesn't take long to realise my students' levels of concentration suffers after lunch. I begin to wonder, did some students eat amnesia custard[31] for lunch? By all appearances, they've forgotten anything I taught them in the morning. Perhaps they feel grateful they were provided with name cards on their desks so at least they can remember something.

A time series graph of their concentration looks something like this:

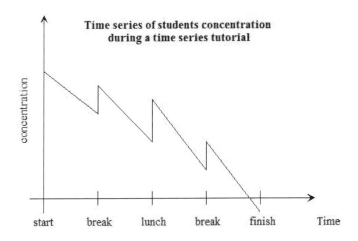

For quieter groups, it is difficult to measure increased quietness without specialist sound detection equipment.

However, all too soon students start participating in a synchronised wave of yawning that stretches from one side of the classroom to the other. If several of them fire out of sequence and yawn in unison, my ears pop from the drop in

---

[31] A clever pun based on Ambrosia custard for those of you who don't live near Devon.

pressure.

As I still have much more to teach these fledglings, I resort to extreme measures to keep them awake.

For example, I act erratically, keeping them on their toes. Though you may say, "How is this erratic behaviour different to your norm, John?'

For example, when we are using Fisher's transformation to test Pearson's correlation coefficient:

$$\frac{\tanh^{-1} r - \tanh^{-1} \rho}{\sqrt{1/(n-3)}} \stackrel{.}{\sim} N(0,1)$$

This requires the use of hyperbolic trigonometric functions, which on a Casio calculator involves pressing the 'hyp' button to access the hyperbolic menu. My explanation goes something like this:

"If you press the hyp button on your calculator, then your calculator will go

WOO HOO!"

Pause while students are treated for heart attacks

"No, no! Not that kind of hype."

If you'd like to fully appreciate the shock felt by my students, I recommend listening to the audio version of this book. Standard disclaimer inserted here. The author cannot be held liable for chest pains, shortness of breath, and/or hospitalisation that might result.

My standard approach, however, is to let the air-conditioning do the dirty work. It's hard to sleep when you're freezing your actuarial assumptions off.

STIMULANTS

Despite students slipping into unconsciousness, I manage to keep going without caffeine or any other stimulants, such as Red Bull energy drinks.

You see, stimulants and I tend to have a little disagreement. After seeing a student crack open a Red Bull halfway through my first ever actuarial exam, I thought to myself, "Now, there's a clever idea!" I duly purchased myself my first ever can of Red Bull to try in my second exam.

I drank maybe a quarter of the can. However, when I phoned my wife after the exam some three hours later, I was still shaking. "It went really well," I told her in my quivery voice. Her perceptiveness as to the cause of my strange manner of speech led her to ask, "Did you have an energy drink?" When I confessed, she kindly realised the best course of action was to lock me out of the house and only allow me back in after hours of vigorous sporting activities with my children. After which, 'normality' should have returned.

But I must confess that the strong negative correlation between the students' energy levels in the afternoon and my own have made me wonder if my descendants were from

Transylvania. But then I remember that correlation is not necessarily causation. I console myself that the fact that this has occurred in every tutorial for more than 20 years is mere coincidence as are my unusually long canine teeth.

As students' concentration dips, so does their ability to work through any exam question whatsoever. And so, I try to encourage such students as much as possible with comments like, "Well done, you've managed to write down the question number. Now on to the next step!"

When I gently address the apparent lack of progress, students often tell me that they are "thinking about it" as if this is meant to reassure me. What were they doing the rest of the day if not thinking?

More worrying than this are those students who are so desperate to avoid writing by this point of the day that they stoop to "discussing it" with their neighbour. How low can actuarial students go that they would debase themselves thus? And what's worse; they publicly engage in such conversation! Good job that there are no young children attending my tutorials who could be traumatised by such scenes. This kind of behaviour should be done behind closed doors. Technically speaking, the door to my room is closed anyhow to keep you-know-who out.

Special shout out to the student who had not written anything. When I questioned him, he responded with the excuse that he was just browsing the questions.

At this point, the tutorial devolves into a "just copy down what I'm writing on the board" session as the mental ability of my attendees has long since flown south for winter.

THE END

I am always impressed that my students are typically so respectful of my time that they want to ensure they don't take more of it than their company has paid for. They are ready to leave the moment the clock strikes 5pm. However, there's always that *one* student who wants to go one step further in their pursuit of not appearing greedy and leaves 30 minutes early.

Some let me know in advance that they've got to catch a train, a plane, or a cold. I think they only say this to spare my feelings. The remaining class outwardly express disapproval whilst inwardly seethe with jealousy at the student's initiative.

In their great travail, they cry out for someone to rescue them from the yoke of statistical slavery and behold there was sent to them a deliverer: Moses the actuarial student cometh forth, demanding that I let his people go.

In the words of Queen, I reply, "I will not let them go...let me go...no, no, no, no, no, oh Mamma Mia, Mamma Mia..."

But then, the clock finally reaches five and it's time to tuck the students into bed and read them an actuarial fairy tale.

And little Red Riding Hood said, 'What lovely Yule-Walker equations you have, Grandma!'

'All the better for solving time series processes, my dear...'"

"See you next time," I say to an empty room; for the students have set a new land speed record for packing up and leaving.

Straight after the tutorial finishes, I send my students a PDF copy of the notes. I just know how eager they will all be to dig into more work on the way home or in that evening.

I confess that this is one of the advantages of creating notes for my class on a computer. When I used flip charts, if anyone wanted to take home my notes, they would need a large suitcase or a team of porters. I honestly had students who wanted to take the flipchart pad home. It was a bit tense if more than one of them wanted the notes, but this was nothing that pistols at dawn couldn't solve.

I actually wonder whether having notes that inconveniently difficult to carry meant that students were more likely to read them again - if only to clear the space in their house. These days, notes are sent through email and they probably just sit there unopened, languishing unloved in the inbox.

As an actuary I like to test things out. And so, on occasion, I'll insert a page in the middle of the notes that asks, "I wonder if anyone actually reads these notes." Mysteriously, no-one has emailed me a response, and so my curiosity remains unsated.

A fun game I like to play (and by fun, I mean actuarial fun and not what the rest of the world might call fun) is to see which student's email account sends the first out-of-office autoreply[32].

Sadly, GDPR means I now have to send the email containing the notes to myself and bcc the students. On the plus side, sending an email to myself fills up my inbox. This makes me feel popular[33] but it is a serious spanner in the world of actuarial dating. For it is a well-known fact that dating anyone in your office is a bad idea. So, tutorials are one of the few times that the introvert actuary gets to meet new people who don't ask, "what is an actuary?" And what better way to start a relationship than to email a fellow student from your tutor group about a question you were having difficulty on?

---

[32] Yes, I know I need to get a life.

[33] Note I said "feel" popular. Remember, feelings don't necessarily line up with facts or indeed anything rational.

THE LAST TUTORIAL

Well, all good things come to an end, which is probably why my tutorials last forever.

After doing a quick check that all students have been equally insulted, I then face the tricky question of how to leave them with something memorable. Since tattoos are probably out of the question, I try to come up with some suitable words that will etch indelibly on their minds.

I used to go for "I hope we never meet again" which probably sounded a bit rude. But we actuaries stridently assert that you should always state your assumptions. These are "as otherwise that means you're retaking this subject or that I'm teaching you CA1/CP1 – neither of which will be a pleasant experience."

But somehow that didn't ring true. For on occasion, I *do* meet students again and when I do, I happily chat to them. I have to admit though, there's always that awkward moment when I can't remember their name. Students also find such chance meetings awkward as well. They don't know how to ask me to stop talking to them whilst they're using the urinal.

So, I then moved to closing my sessions with: "I'll see you on the pass lists! And if you're not there, then I'll find out where you live and hunt you down like the dirty dogs that you are."

Repeated testing showed that this sentence was more intimidating than threatening them with stealing their cat, thus encouraging them to work harder.

However, due to "reputational risk", the Profession no longer releases public pass lists. For example, two students might have the same name and one might have failed while the other passed and we won't know which. Or maybe one student could have requested, under GDPR, to have their name removed from these public lists and everyone would therefore assume that person had failed, rather than they were just a snowflake.

It's such a shame that no-one came up with the idea of displaying the student's ARNs (Actuarial Reference Number) next to their names to help distinguish between them. Heck, even actuarial-lookup keeps confusing me with John Weng Kong Lee from Hong Kong:

> This individual may have registered for exams under different names. The following person(s) may also refer to the person currently displayed:
> - John Weng Kong Lee, FIA

http://www.actuarial-lookup.co.uk/results/ykbdrc

I'm pretty sure GDPR would be fine with the website announcing, "The following students have declined to allow their results to be made public…"

So now I face a future with no way of knowing if my students have actually passed or not, though the more pressing issue is not having a funny ending to my last tutorial.

So, my latest iteration of my final words is: "Sadly, I won't have any idea if you've passed unless you send me money through the post to say thank you." However, the students I so far have tried this on have all laughed nervously. Presumably. it's just because they're not sure exactly how much money is appropriate to send me as a Thank You. So, I guess I need to work on making my closing remarks clearer in the future.

PART 8

The after math

LIFE BEYOND THE TUTORIAL

With the end of such an epic era, some tutor groups might feel a strange urge to prolong the last precious moments they have with their beloved tutor and so invite me to the pub.

Don't look so shocked. It has happened.

Admittedly, only three times in more than 20 years, which makes it about as common as stock market crashes. But strangely enough, these events are not as widely reported in the media as a crash.

Some Dublin students were the first to ever invite me to the pub after our last tutorial. Actually, I think they asked to go to the pub *instead* of attending the tutorial, but I thought it best to wait until I had actually attempted to teach them something. I was pleasantly surprised to discover that they did not invite me along in the hopes I would pay for all their drinks. I was further surprised that one of the students offered to buy me a drink.

I confess I didn't order a Guinness. It's a massive outlier from my drinking experience and so I opted for half a cider. The

Irish student who had offered to buy me a drink looked horrified, protesting, "I wouldn't be seen dead ordering *half* a pint!" and she bought me a pint of cider instead. I don't remember much more of that evening, but that's because of my age. Honest.

TUTORIAL FEEDBACK

After the tutorials have finished, students are sent a feedback questionnaire in which they are asked to rate the tutor on their quality of teaching followed by a "how can the tutor improve?" comment box.

For me, the absolute worst kind of feedback is when they score my teaching as average and then leave the "how can the tutor improve" box blank.

Clearly I'm destined to be average for all my life.

THE OTHER JOHN

Now many years ago, when students posted back their feedback forms, my boss would analyse and present the summary in a spreadsheet. This led to much rivalry between tutors to see who got the coveted top tutor score. This spurred us[34] on to sabotage our colleagues' tutorials so that we would come up on top. Oops, I meant to say, it spurred us on to improve our teaching methods. I can't think why we moved to private feedback.

Back then, however, my boss would pick out a few comments to share with us all. One year, he reported, "This feedback for John's tutorial was interesting," and then read out a student's comment which described how hot they though the tutor was[35].

I was dumfounded.

"I've never had anyone say that about me!" I responded to the room packed full of tutors.

---

[34] Okay, maybe it was just me...

[35] I'd love to tell you the exact phrase, but sadly the lawyers said that funniness isn't a good enough reason to breach GDPR. And I thought only actuaries had no sense of humour.

To which my boss replied, "No, not you John! The other John."

For there is not one, but two tutors named John at the company. And the other John, with his rugged good looks, is without doubt, more attractive than me and was (rather obviously now I think back on it) the recipient of such praise. However, it never hurts to dream unless you are a sleepwalker and you end up falling down the stairs.

In fact, my children often ask me how on earth I managed to marry their beautiful mother. I wisely reply, "Never underestimate the power of humour to win the heart of a woman." And then add, "Or how previously dating a deadbeat boyfriend causes a woman to lower her standards."

However, that being said, my wife still finds my jokes funny, even after more than 20 years of marriage. Though I suspect some of that is due to the memory issues which result from her disability[36].

---

[36] For the person who is offended by this joke: The reality of living with my wife's increasing disability is that joking about it together is part of what makes it bearable. Please don't take that away from us. Okay, serious footnote over. Back to the jokes.

THE COMMENTS

Well, seeing as you have spent your hard-earned cash on my book, I'd love to share with you some of the highlights of actual feedback I've received over the years. However, the lawyers gave me that evil stare again. So, let me give you a generic summary of the gist of the comments.

- Some commented that they were surprised by how useful or interesting the tutorials were. To be honest so was I, but I'll try harder to meet their expectations in the future.

- Some loved my jokes, whereas others felt it necessary to add that they only laughed because the jokes were so bad. Whereas others were upset that such frivolous jokes took up valuable teaching time. Clearly, they failed to realise that I was teaching them to have a sense of humour. I will have to try harder in the future.

- Some used the comment box to point out how they shouldn't have to be in a tutorial with less-prepared students, whereas others who attended 2-day tutorials complained that it was all too rushed and demanded that I should use some kind of quantum field to alter the space-time continuum so I could teach the same amount as the 3-day tutorials they didn't want to pay for.

- And finally, one student reported how I gave everyone a personal touch, which led to extensive police questioning over any inappropriate behaviour.

EMAIL HELP

I encourage students to email me with all their queries.

I tell them that I used to email my tutor loads when I was a student and it helped me so much that I want payback. Or I want to pay it forward or something like that. One of the two; I get them confused. I reassure them that I have never say to anyone "Stop asking questions!" Although, there was that one student to whom I said, "I don't think you should be an actuary." It was like their fourth question about stem-and-leaf diagrams. Seriously!

Sometimes, you have to tell people the truth or they might end up all bitter and twisted some 16 years down the line, still struggling to qualify, and then suing the Profession for "hurt feelings"[37].

You see, students emailing me is a win-win scenario:

1. I help them understand, they pass the exams, and they then feel so thankful that they send me money through

---

[37] Did that last sentence seem oddly specific? Then let me assure you that any resemblance to trainee actuaries living and dead is purely coincidental. Honest.

the post. Or at the very least, buy this book and leave a glowing review on Amazon or Goodreads.

2. As my inbox fills, I feel like I'm really popular, all without me having to send emails to myself. In addition, I get to spend time answering students' queries rather than doing all those other boring office jobs that cause me to sink (further) into insanity.

However, no matter how many emails come through, I always end questioning the amount. Do too few emails mean that my students are not doing any work? Do they have questions but are refusing to ask me out of spite? Perhaps my explanation was just so good in class that students have no questions at all. Or perhaps not.

Do too many emails mean that they think that I'm approachable? Or that they're lazy or that my explanations suck? Or did they just sign me up on spam lists?

NICE EMAILS

One of the best parts of my job would be when students send me money through the post. I've yet to experience this, but I have every confidence that when it happens it will be totally amazing.

However, the next best part is when students send me nice emails. It's even better when they do so, unsolicited. I must confess that the whole begging thing is becoming quite demeaning.

I store those little treasures of email in a folder titled 'Nice Emails', and I read them from time to time to cheer my soul when I'm feeling low. Whilst including these 200 gushing emails would make me feel better, I suspect it would not be that interesting for anyone else, except for the GDPR lawyers. So, here are two emails that made me laugh, feel all squiggly inside, and whose authors gave me permission to include in this book:

"Hi John, thanks for the fab tutorials. I am sure I will see you for the next round on a re sit, ha."

and:

"I tried to fail so I could experience those puns again, unfortunately I passed."

Special shout out to:

- Raquel who sent me a picture of a chocolate cake which was almost as good as the real thing.

- Chris, to whom I said, "If you pass all four exams, I'll buy you a pint." It's been 4 years and I think he's forgotten.

- And Naeem who was very gracious about the money I sent him for his kind words that got mysteriously lost in the post. Honest.

Then there is a specific kind of email I receive that I'm not quite sure whether it's a compliment or not.

It's when students ask me what tutorials I'm teaching next session.

Without any assumptions, I don't know whether they are asking so they can avoid my tutorials, or because they'd like to be hear the same jokes all over again.

Remember kids, actuarial assumptions can stop needless suffering.

CARDS

Back in 1997, snail mail was so dull and emails were super special as you might only get one or maybe two a day. Now some 20 years later, everything has reversed. It's now super special to receive something through the post from students unless of course it's another one of those anonymous threatening letters.

More than 20 years of dedicated teaching and sacrificing myself to help students succeed in their careers and become rich and famous has resulted in two cards and one out-of-date Christmas pudding delivered through the post[38].

Three gifts in over 20 years! That makes them about as common as me getting invited to the pub after a tutorial, still sadly unreported in the media despite being nearly as exciting as a visit from our beloved Queen.

Both cards came from students who worked in the government actuary's department, thus leading me to conclude that it must be a nice place to work. It tempted me to give up my tutoring ways and get an office job there. But then, I

---

[38] It still tasted fine though. Hey, don't judge me! I'm not wasting any food.

actually spend a day in my office and realised that I would go quite, quite mad if I worked in an office full-time.

Well here's a picture of those special cards to end this book with:

Do these cards I've given pride of place to on my desk warm the cockles of your heart? Are you moved by the story of the poor actuarial tutor who only received two cards over a 20-year period? Would you be prepared to sponsor a tutor for the low low price of only £10 a month? Cash, debit, and all major credit cards accepted. We also accept part-exchange on Excel macros.

Remember: A tutor is for life – not just until you pass the exam.

Make the difference in a tutor's life today!

PART 9

All that stuff that goes at the end

REVIEW

Thank you for buying this book[39]. By doing so, you are encouraging John to write more books. This keeps him off the streets, which is safer for society.

Also, John's psychoanalyst said that receiving positive reviews on Amazon improves John's fragile sense of wellbeing. Since, as an actuary, you are clearly an upstanding member of society, I know that you will come to the aid of a fellow actuary in distress by making a five-minute sacrifice to write such a review.

You can even use this link to take you straight to the book page[40]:

getBook.at/ActuarialTutor

---

[39] At least, I assuming you've bought it and you aren't one of those cheapskates reading it in the bookshop instead.

[40] I know what you're thinking, "What a helpful and altruistic guy.."

AM I MISSING SOMETHING?

Well, the obvious answer is "Yes John, you're a couple of sandwiches short of a picnic."

But seriously, if there is an amusing story, joke, or anecdote that I've forgotten due to age and actuarial exams destroying my ability to remember anything non-exam related, then drop me an email at **ActuarialTutorUK@gmail.com**.

I'll include it in the next edition[41].

---

[41] Unless, of course, I get struck off by the Profession for having a sense of humour or I forget, due to age and actuarial exams destroying my ability to...what was I saying?

PLEASE SIR, CAN I HAVE SOME MORE?

If your standards are so low that you think that this book is amusing, then you can either seek help from a qualified medical practitioner or you can follow me on Amazon to get notified when I finally get around to writing the sequel, *"The Secret Life of Actuaries."*

If you're also a Christian, then you might be interested to know that I've also written more than 10 Christian parody and satire books under a pseudonym. Drop me an email at **ActuarialTutorUK@gmail.com**, and I'll discretely send you the details.

I also run the Christian meme page "Not the Bible" and the Christian Satirical News website "The Salty Cee" if you need daily reminders of why I need prayer.

ABOUT THE AUTHOR

John was born at a very young age with his umbilical cord wrapped around his neck. At first, it appeared that no lasting damage had been done, but as he grew, it became clear that his sense of humour had been damaged irreparably.

John studied mathematics at Oxford University where he also trained as a teacher. Despite this, he still refers to himself in the third person. Whilst there, he performed stand-up comedy as part of the Oxford Revue. Making audiences laugh was too easy, so he progressed to greater challenges: making maths interesting and making boring actuaries laugh.

When he's not wrestling with his work-life balance or literally wrestling with his four children, he's wrestling with writing funny words on a page in his cramped study.

John lives with his family near Oxford, England where he wonders how his wife still finds the same jokes funny after more than 20 years of marriage.

Why are you still reading? This book has finished.

Look, if you're that desperate to read more, then just buy one of my other books rather than hunting around for scraps of funniness at the back of this book.

Printed in Great Britain
by Amazon